WHAT PEOPLE ARE
SAYING ABOUT PAULINE

I have known Pauline Nguyen for over five years on a personal and professional level. Pauline has touched my life in numerous profound ways. Pauline's wisdom, knowledge and presence are a direct reflection of her exceptional character. Other than Pauline's extraordinary business acumen, the trait I love the most about Pauline is her no BS approach to all aspects of life. Pauline is THE MOST focused and disciplined person I know. Pauline is all about finding the solution to get results in a way that serves the greater good of all involved. Pauline has taught me many lessons over the years of our relationship and my greatest lesson from being in her circle and presence comes from her ability to openly love, accept and honour who she is at her core without any distractions by the external world.

Her heart to serve is endless, her presence commanding, and her intent is always pure to serve those around her to unleash the inner greatness within them.

I've not met a speaker, trainer or authority who can communicate and extract greatness from people the way that Pauline can. She is a true gift to humanity.

Pauline from my heart to yours, THANK YOU for being you, and helping to lead me back to the essence of who I truly I am.

Kim Burke, developer of the Make It Happen Method, entrepreneur and investor

'Status quo'... these were two words that I used to be comfortable with until I met Pauline. My days are now framed differently. She has taught me to have a mindset of what my tomorrow will bring or, better yet, what will I bring to my tomorrow. What was I grateful for today, and from lessons learned, how can I be an improved version of myself tomorrow, refining the relations of those in my orbit?

These are lessons that vibrate through my day, largely due to listening to and watching Pauline. I had never encountered a person who not only takes nothing for granted, but also learns from each and every experience to ensure she evolves and transforms the current version of herself into a superior and greater BEING.

Pauline will not sacrifice an iota of herself or her beliefs in favour of what society may at that point dictate it 'should' be. She is a warrior, pushing humanity towards a true and virtuous conscience. I'm unsure as to how many lives she may have had prior to this, but in the two years I've had the pleasure of knowing her, she would have achieved more than some do in a lifetime. That in and of itself is a lesson I also cherish.

Dean Perlman, Annex Group

Pauline has been my coach and mentor for the last four years. She is without a doubt, the biggest disruptor and most powerful influence in my life. She takes you to another level with her presence and her energy. She makes it very easy to open up to her and share. Her mission to live her most authentic self is shown through her words and actions every day. Her calibre, her credibility and her influence is incredible. I am incredibly honoured and privileged that she has taught me so much. She has made a profound impact not only in my professional career, but also in all areas of my life. She has made a massive impact on my health, my mindset as well as my spirituality. She has lifted my game of life. Sometimes it is difficult to listen contently because Pauline is not afraid to speak her truth, she tells me what I need to hear, not what I want to hear. She constantly pushes me to always challenge the status quo so that I can be better than before. Firm but fair – no bullshit, is the name of her game.

Kevin Phi Vu Ly, entrepreneur and Founder, Brewristers Coffee

The things that spring to mind when I think about a Spiritual Entrepreneur are integrity, purpose and vision, and Pauline Nguyen has all three in abundance. There are people who you meet and you know in that immediate instance that it's a game changer and life is about to get a whole lot more interesting.

It was certainly a game changer when I met Pauline. I have now worked with Pauline for the last two years and it never ceases to amaze me her ability to anticipate and expand ahead of the pack, to lead and mentor me by example and also through sage advice at the right time.

Pauline truly walks her talk and has been practising what she teaches for years. She is a master at what she does. The changes I've seen in myself and the projects that I have launched successfully since being in her space have been exponential. She saw my potential before I saw it myself and her belief and support has been unwavering.

Dr Maria Zuschmann, integrative chiropractor and Director, Inner Edge Wellness; Founder, The Queen of Stress

I was an absolute novice in knowing the real me. Spiritual was a word that scared me and I pictured it as happy clappies singing to me. Then Pauline rocked into my life.

Working with Pauline and having the fortune to diving deep in both our worlds is irreplaceable. The tools Pauline has given me to hack my spiritual self are nothing short of a gift. Pauline's candid and direct, no bullshit approach is refreshing and authentic. I have been able to advance in my business and personal success due to knowing this spiritual ninja. Pauline gives me a masterclass in no bullshit every time I see her.

Darren McKenzie, CEO, McKenzie Partners

Pauline is our generation's heart, soul and fire. Her light shines bright, leading the way with care and grace. She challenges you to shed. She pushes you to invite more. She compels you to put in the work. Every day. She places light in the dark that illuminates the beauty of the ALL. As a fellow entrepreneur on a mission to transform the world, this is what I need in a leader. Not more 'you should do this', or 'you gotta buy me' that we are bombarded with every single day, that feeds doubt and scarcity. Rewiring how we see ourselves, how we experience our connection with this planet and each other, and changing the mechanics of doing business every day is desperately needed for us all to level up and push humanity truly forward and higher. Pauline is a living and breathing example of this, and is here on a soul purpose to invite us all on that journey, together. And I am in.

I have known, worked with and had the pleasure of being mentored by Pauline for over ten years. She truly sits among the great spiritual leaders of our time and I will forever be a student of the Way of the Spiritual Entrepreneur.

Jessica Kiely, Chief Wanderess, Wanderess Beauty

Where does one even start to talk about Pauline Nguyen? Pauline is probably the most interesting person I have ever met in my entire life. I feel so incredibly privileged to know her. She is the true definition of a Spiritual Entrepreneur. Pauline operates at a higher level than anyone else I know. This incredible human has the innate ability to reframe your perspectives, challenge your thinking, and deepen your understanding of self and the universe – all in the space of one conversation. I feel incredibly blessed every time I spend time with Pauline. She has opened my eyes to the fact that there is so much more to spirituality than I would have ever have realised, or have ever known to actually go looking for. She has reframed so many of my perspectives on not only myself but also the world around us. To spend time with Pauline is to come out a better version of yourself than you went in with. She questions and she challenges. She knows exactly what to say at exactly the right moment to expand your knowledge, your understanding and your self-development journey. Her mentorship has escalated me to a whole new level of consciousness. Blending science and spirituality, Pauline is unapologetically working on raising the collective consciousness, and I for one want to be on that journey. Anyone who has the privilege and opportunity to be anywhere in her orbit or her field, please, just do it because you 100 per cent will not regret it.

Kerry Dover, Director and Marketing Strategist, Momentum Architects

Pauline emanates authenticity. Pauline is someone who shows up day after day to help people elevate so they can become the most honest and real version of themselves. She has an extraordinary gift that lies beyond the intellect that inspires and empowers people to interact in life in a joyful and courageous way that encourages you to get out of your comfort zone. Each time I see her, she changes my life a little more as she always teaches me something new. After spending time with her, I often think to myself, *How do I find more people like Pauline to surround myself with?*

Ben Handler, Co-Founder and former CEO of Australia's largest property buyer's agency

My world simply shifted when I met Pauline and had the honour of connecting with her particularly at one of the most difficult times of my life. Pauline's strength of being and sage presence somehow made me strengthen the very essence of who I am as a person and how I choose my life to be. Without unnecessary words to clutter space and time, Pauline repeatedly held a safe place for me, altered my self-perception, and alleviated my resolve to not accept the constraints others placed on me. I reflect often on the time with Pauline and lean into the spirit and intention of those times. It stays with me, guides me and inspires me more than I have words. She replenished my soul; always strong and direct but never arrogant. Pauline has a humility that is palpable and her words make you sit up straighter and pay attention to life!

Margo Ward, Founder and CEO, KidsXpress

From the moment I connected with Pauline, her spiritual perspective and philosophy started to change me. It happened slowly through the reading of her words and the watching of her example. Watching the creative, impassioned strides she made in her own life and the huge impact she was making to others inspired me to take control of my own in a way I have never done before. Through Pauline's guidance I have learnt to love and accept myself completely, to embrace the life both behind me and ahead of me, while appreciating the very moment I exist in now. Through doing so I have not only learnt to love and accept others in the same way but I have also discovered the true purpose deep within myself and I am now chasing it with everything I have got. Thank you, Pauline, for these gifts and so much more. I would recommend your wisdom and guidance to anyone, at any time or stage in their life.

Kel Butler, author, speaker and podcaster ('Listen Up', 'Writes4Women')

Pauline Nguyen takes a very holistic and honest view of coaching. She is direct and impactful. For those who are looking to learn, grow and change at a rapid pace, Pauline's style is effective and efficient. She doesn't like to muck around. From my own personal experience, Pauline is really about focusing on the ability to speak the truth, which, ultimately, is what generates long-term results in people's lives. In a culture dominated by hierarchy that is influenced by public opinion, Pauline implements principles based on staying true to one's core. She encourages us to find the courage to be our authentic self and engender our core values. This in turn provides the stem for the growth in our confidence and our state … always coming from a place of congruence from within. Pauline will call out the truth when needed and confront the blockages immediately in a format and platform as she sees fit without any recrimination or self-interest in protecting herself or how she is seen. Her true accountability and satisfaction is in delivering results. As a professional, she only feels completeness when there is breakthrough. From experience, her motivation in collecting the monetary transaction is only secondary to her client's success in implementing the tangible results into their lives.

Donny Chien, entrepreneur and Founder, Y Waste

Not many leaders have walked the talk, and experienced what they preach. They haven't taken the road less travelled, yet chase the glory and limelight for self-gain.

Pauline is the real thing! Decades of investing in herself, exploring, experiencing, unlocking new levels of her spiritual self and helping others do the same, not through text books but through personal experience and dedication. If you want to level up and become a more enlightened entrepreneur, with more joy, flow and purpose, then I definitely believe Pauline is a level beyond what you have ever experienced before.

Paul Shepherd, digital and health entrepreneur

THE WAY OF THE SPIRITUAL ENTREPRENEUR

The 7 Secrets to Becoming Fearless,
Stress Free and Unshakable in
Business and in Life

PAULINE NGUYEN

First published in 2019 by Pauline Nguyen

Reprinted in July 2019

ISBN: 978-0-6484024-5-9

Printed in Australia by McPherson's Printing Group
Project management and text design by Michael Hanrahan Publishing
Cover design by Peter Reardon

Disclaimer: The material in this publication is of the nature of general comment only, and does not represent professional advice. It is not intended to provide specific guidance for particular circumstances and it should not be relied on as the basis for any decision to take action or not take action on any matter which it covers. Readers should obtain professional advice where appropriate, before making any such decision. To the maximum extent permitted by law, the author and publisher disclaim all responsibility and liability to any person, arising directly or indirectly from any person taking or not taking action based on the information in this publication.

For my son, Jethro Heathcliff Jensen,
who is everything that is beautiful about me.

ABOUT THE AUTHOR

Pauline Nguyen – Award Winning Author, highly sought after International Speaker and one of the most grounded Spiritual Entrepreneurs around the globe. —The Huffington Post

Pauline is one of Australia's most successful entrepreneurs – but with difference. She is inspiration with substance. She teaches with warmth and humour, telling her own story of what can be achieved through key alignment of thoughts and intentions. She has a high-performing Western business background combined with an Eastern slant of spirituality.

Pauline is a best-selling author and award-winning businesswoman – and her achievements are all the more impressive for her having escaped Vietnam on a boat and survived a Thai refugee camp. She has overcome these adverse beginnings to transform her approach to success by re-engineering her beliefs, questioning the status quo and hacking cultural norms.

Pauline's unique life experiences have given her a distinctive insight into the minds of individuals and businesses alike, allowing her to pass on the invaluable skills of self-mastery, courage, resilience and grit. As Pauline says, 'If we can learn the tools of self-mastery, we can better practice the art of influence over others.'

Pauline's achievements are many. She is the owner of Red Lantern, the most awarded Vietnamese restaurant in the world. In 2012, she won the Australian Telstra Business Award for Medium Business.

But that is only the tip of the iceberg when it comes to Pauline's achievements; her memoir, *Secrets of the Red Lantern*, has been critically acclaimed around the world and appeared in numerous bestseller lists. She holds a BA in Communications from the University of Technology, Sydney, and in 2008 won Newcomer Writer of the Year at the Australian Book Industry Awards.

Pauline has achieved outstanding success as an entrepreneur, author, businesswoman and acclaimed speaker, and also has the skills to connect with her audience and her clients in a profound way – she helps awaken and focus people to change their own story for a better future. Pauline is an original 'Rare Bird' – one of Australia's top 50 influential female entrepreneurs – and is included in Blackwell and Hobday's global recognition of *200 Women Who Will Change the Way You See the World*.

When Pauline talks of commitment driving outcomes, people listen.

CONTENTS

The better we know ourselves, the less we fear change in our world.

The better we know ourselves, the less we fear others.

The better we know ourselves, the less we fear ourselves and our own power.

—Gregg Braden, Science and Spirituality Conference, Nanaimo, British Columbia 2018

MY GUARANTEE

It is my pure joy that this book has found you.

I know people normally choose books. This time, however, this book has chosen you. And it's by no coincidence. The fact that you now have this book means I have written it just for you, to give you the awakening you need in your life at the very time you need it.

Neither of us knew this finding each other would happen. But it has.

It is our destiny to meet this way, for we have many life lessons to learn from each other. And so today, we begin our journey together. We will refer to this journey as The Way of The Spiritual Entrepreneur.

Purposely woven within these pages are the intimate stories of my tumultuous life. I will share my hard-earned lessons and the secrets that have emerged from them. Also included among these pages are the whispers of the wisdom of the ages that I wish to gift to you.

The lessons I share with you have not come easy to me. I have fought for them at great cost and the outcome is the many disciplines that I have discovered throughout this lifetime – the secrets that have allowed me to become the woman that my destiny has called me to be.

Why has this book chosen you? Because the Universe knows you have a hunger in you. A burning desire to be more, do more, have more and give more than what the status quo requires of you.

This book has further chosen you because you have questions that have yet to be answered and you are not afraid to ask them. This book has chosen you because you are either an aspiring or already established entrepreneur searching for the ultimate goal. You're asking, 'What's next? What's the next level?' Or you are a Seeker who yearns to learn 'the way with greater meaning'.

By taking this time to learn the seven secrets outlined in this book, you will understand what it means to become a Spiritual Entrepreneur. Adopting the Way of the Spiritual Entrepreneur will help you remove the stress and struggle that comes with being in your own business and 'walking the road less travelled'.

How do I know all this? I have met many people just like you. I choose to surround myself with people like you. I know who you are. I know how you think. I know what you feel.

It's in my blood. My parents were entrepreneurs. My brothers are entrepreneurs. Some of the most successful entrepreneurs in my universe are my teachers and my friends.

So I know what's inside you at a cellular level. You have a deep yearning to be happy, fulfilled and rewarded for the great efforts and sacrifices you make. I know it because I have walked this path.

THE ROAD LESS TRAVELLED

Entrepreneurs are the eternal warriors of the world. We take the hard road. We are the outliers – the ones who don't fit in, the ones who have divorced ourselves from the crowd, the ones who have freed ourselves from the conformity of others.

We are often accused as being obsessive, single-minded, unreasonable and irrational. We are monomaniacal about the things that matter most. Our spirit thrives on meeting the next challenge. It is who we are. It is in our DNA. We take huge risks – some calculated, some not so calculated. In our world, a lot is always at stake. But we are the delusional optimists. We understand that every slight, every adversity, every challenge is gold. We use these as fuel to become the person we are destined to be.

As entrepreneurs, the common bond we all share is this: the deep need for self-determination, the need to create, the need to take risks to achieve something more, the need to solve problems, and to be part of the change we would like to see in the world. Governments have rarely succeeded in solving society's problems. It is businesses and entrepreneurs who have made the greatest impact and pushed the greatest change. And this is because we all share unrelenting drive. We have great vision and, most of all, we want to lead and succeed from the front. We want to be a good example to those around us and show people what is possible – and not accept the impossible.

While this is a noble pursuit, and one which entrepreneurs cherish and live for, it is also highly challenging in many ways. The challenges affect us right down to our very core.

The life of a business owner or entrepreneur requires many things – including courage, determination, resilience, persistence, grit, creativity, flexibility, commitment and self-belief. It requires the gumption to go against the grain, ignoring the opinions of others, and to be headstrong when there is little or no support anywhere in sight.

This is not easy, and few things in life will ever be as confronting, challenging and all-consuming as building a business.

While great rewards are gained if we succeed, this success comes with a heavy burden. In 98 per cent of cases, we get so single-minded, so hungry to achieve, that we don't fully know or appreciate until much later the hidden and sometimes heavy price we have paid, and the struggle we need to endure to achieve this success.

I am sure you have heard people in business say, 'If I'd known how hard this would be, I would never have done it.' Perhaps you have felt this way yourself – and never a truer statement was spoken!

COUNTING YOUR LOSSES

For the already established entrepreneur, I know how hard you have had to work and how much you have had to sacrifice to get to where you are today. I know about the sleepless nights you have had to endure and the relationships that you have had to forgo. I know about the ridicule and the criticism that others have dumped upon you. I know about cash flow stress, the pressures of the competition and the imposter monster that keeps you awake at night.

But we do it anyway and we work hard and we push and commit to our quest day after day, year after year, many times fighting for every inch we gain, despite all the odds stacked against us.

But if we are not careful, we also lose much along this journey.

What do we lose? In many cases, we lose ourselves and our most valued relationships. We lose our time and the many other interests we have in life. Sadly, in many cases, we even lose our health. We get caught up in the struggle to avoid failure. To win and succeed at all costs – with no guarantees and no safety net.

And, if and when we finally 'get there', when we are able to lift our heads to breathe and look around at what we have achieved, what do we find? We find that the very thing we set out to achieve has eluded us. At the end of this long road, 'success', whether big or small, is not what we thought, hoped or imagined it would be. And in many cases, this discovery comes too late.

I look around at the entrepreneurs in my world and many of them are extremely successful. That doesn't mean that they are not suffering. So many suffer quietly and silently on their own. It hurts my heart to see them in pain. Many are too embarrassed, ashamed or unwilling to admit weakness to share these fears, doubts and failures with their friends, their family, their children and their work colleagues.

They suffer in silence putting on a brave face. This is ultimately what causes many to have nervous breakdowns, commit suicide or end up in jail. Their pride and loneliness means they simply cannot face up to the reality of failure – or their perceived idea of failure.

They would rather hide this failure, implode, or steal from others to mask it publically.

Lack of success jolts their self-esteem. Negative assessment from others makes them feel 'less than' or looked down upon and unloved. And so, they work even harder and try even harder – but they still don't make it. And this vicious cycle ends up destroying their lives, their marriages and their relationships with their children – all through scarcity of time, lack of support, lack of knowledge and lack of money.

If we have been lucky along the entrepreneurial journey, we might have acquired, or be on the way to acquiring, the finer material things we thought would make us happy. By doing so, we may at first feel we have achieved the 'dream' we have been sold for so many years.

We have sacrificed much to get here. But now that we have 'arrived', we are disillusioned and we still yearn for what is missing – adventure, a sense of meaning, a sense of purpose and connection. In essence, we are missing happiness with who we have become and what we have achieved, and respect from those around us.

So, what is the answer? And where do we find this missing piece?

The missing piece is this book. *The Way of the Spiritual Entrepreneur* is the new frontier in the science of achievement – because the old ways are no longer working for so many of us.

I wrote this book because I want to create something tangible that my fellow entrepreneurs can take away, absorb and action for themselves. I wrote this book to help you to understand that in your everyday life, opportunities for happiness and fulfilment are staring you in the face.

I want to awaken you, and help you to realise that you already have inside of you the means to get there. Yes, the place of happiness, success and contentment is hidden in plain sight – the best place to hide something so valuable. And that hidden place is right there inside of you. It has always been there, but we have ignored this over and over by buying into someone else's dream and someone else's idea of success.

BUYING INTO SOMEONE ELSE'S DREAM!

If you are ready, it is now time to honour yourself and become truly happy and fulfilled. If you are ready, it is time for a change, a new way, a better way. To honour you and go after the things that truly matter. It's time to take a new path, a true path for you, not for someone else as you may have done for so many years. It's time to put your fear aside and be true to yourself.

I am not suggesting this means a huge change. I am not going to tell you to give your career and all your possessions away and escape to some Himalayan mountain or sit by the seashore chanting for days on end. Definitely not. I am suggesting you take an easier, more fulfilling approach, and a more spiritual approach to your life.

I believe that today, a different kind of suffering has been misdiagnosed as psychological suffering. So many are suffering but it is not psychological suffering – it is spiritual suffering. Indeed, a spiritual crisis is happening at the moment.

I must clear up any confusion that spirituality is connected with religion. I believe that spirituality does not need religion. It is religion that needs spirituality.

To be 'in spirit' means to be inspired, and to perform all tasks and live our lives from a place of inspiration and from a higher mind. Spirituality does not come from religion; it comes from our soul. Spirituality is not theology or ideology. Spirituality is about self-realisation, self-determination, self-actualisation and, ultimately, self-transcendence. Spirituality is about mastering our thoughts, our behaviours and our emotions.

Spiritual Entrepreneurs understand that we only have control over four things in our life – the thoughts we think, the images we visualise, the people we associate with and the actions we take. The purpose of this book is to empower you with new ways of thinking – and new reasons to think differently – so that you have a deeper understanding of yourself and your part in this world, bringing harmony to your home, your life and business.

The Way of the Spiritual Entrepreneur will give you a new, fresh path to becoming truly inspired, authentic and greatly admired because what you will attain will be far more valuable than money. You will attain peace, contentment, fulfilment and true freedom from financial constraints, stress and worry. You will live with love, passion, energy and unbounding enthusiasm naturally and authentically. Most of all, you will be true to yourself.

This book provides simple steps to help you dig deep into the source of your happiness – one that will define you for who you really are. These steps can work in with your current circumstance to help you to make the changes that will allow you to have it all – and there is nothing wrong with wanting to have it all. Abundance is your birthright.

Scattered throughout these pages are also numerous quotes from spectacular minds. I love quotes. Quotes are bite-size nuggets of wisdom and inspiration that, in this age of information overload, provide a moment's peaceful respite and reflection. A well-timed quote can unlock doorways in our hearts and minds, providing just what we need to know at the moment we read it.

Spiritual Entrepreneurship is a new way of being, not doing. The Spiritual Entrepreneur dedicates their mastery and training to LIFE, placing emphasis on their mind, their body, their breath and their emotions, so that they can 'show up' in the face of any adversity – and be fearless, stress free and unshakable. Happiness alone is no longer such a great orientation. Fearlessness is a much more powerful trait. Where fear resides there is gold. These seven secrets will show you how to develop emotional mastery and remain unshakable where X marks the spot. This book is written with one purpose in mind: to empower you in the choices that lead to more freedom, more peacefulness and more joy in a rapidly changing world.

The Way of the Spiritual Entrepreneur is about getting good at LIFE.

Whether you are new to the business world or an already established entrepreneur, adopting the Way of the Spiritual Entrepreneur will enhance the way you operate and navigate the ever-changing circumstances of business and life. My methods and the philosophy that fuels them will transform you in ways you currently cannot imagine possible. You will have the tools to show up more relaxed, more content, more in tune and more attuned with your life – and at your very best for those who rely on you.

YOUR NEW HOME IS A PLACE OF TRUE FREEDOM

One of the biggest challenges for an entrepreneur in today's game is association. The challenge of association we face is that we become the environment we are a part of. We become our associations. We become our conversations. Our environment becomes us and we become our environment. We must choose them well. And so, I ask you: what is the cost of your current association? What is the cost in the lack of power in the people that you run with? What is the cost of remaining in the place where you cannot be truly free?

The Spiritual Entrepreneur community that we have built has become a sanctuary for many. It is the place of belonging that lonely entrepreneurs have been looking for. It is a 'home' to share experiences that previously could not be talked about. It is a place where you are not allowed to hide in the corner and deal with your problems alone.

It is my guarantee that with the implementation of the seven secrets contained in this book, and the support of our community, your transformation cannot be reversed. There is no turning back. You cannot un-know what you will now know. It is my guarantee that you will be 100 per cent more determined to manifest your deepest heart's desire and your soul's strongest calling to design the abundant life that is your birthright.

This is the Way of the Spiritual Entrepreneur.

INTRODUCTION

*To become a master of our thoughts and emotions, like the
Phoenix we need to be able to sit in the discomfort of the
fire. Sitting in the fire is both the process and the initiation.*
—Dr Joe Dispenza

I know what it's like to start from nothing.

My family and I are boat people; refugees who escaped Vietnam
after the war. When Saigon fell to communist rule in 1975, my
father realised he had no choice but to escape Vietnam … and the
only way that he could do this was to build a boat and smuggle
himself and his family out to sea. I was three years old at the time
and my brother Lewis was two.

My grandmother begged him not to leave. She couldn't understand
how a parent would want to risk their children perishing out to
sea. But my father is a very determined man. He stands at just five
foot one, a little shorter than myself, but what he lacks in inches he
makes up for in courage and determination – and he had already
made up his mind. He would rather die trying than risk imprison-
ment or, a fate far worse, the re-education camps. 'It's not enough
that they want to take our freedom,' he would tell me. 'They want
to take our thoughts as well.' He was also determined that if we
died, we would all die together.

So, in October 1977, armed with only a rudimentary map and a
compass to guide him, he steered our tiny vessel out into the South
China Sea. We spent our days drifting and waiting and praying.

We prayed that a foreign ship might come to save us. We prayed that we might find friendly shores. We prayed that the pirates wouldn't attack and rape us, and we prayed that our supplies would not run out. But our prayers were not always answered. Ship after ship after ship ignored our SOS, the most basic distress code of the sea. At gunpoint, a group of Malaysian soldiers pushed us off supposed friendly shores.

We ended up in Thailand, where we spent a horrific year within the barbed wire confines of the Dinh Dieng refugee camp. It was within the walls of this camp that my mother gave birth to my brother Luke. In 1978, Australia finally accepted us. The Fraser Government housed us at Westbridge Migrant Hostel. My father then quickly found a job working on the production line at the Sunbeam Factory in Campsie. Sunbeam gave him the graveyard shift from 2 pm to 2 am and gave him all the jobs that nobody wanted.

Like many entrepreneurs, I grew up in a tough environment. My family came into this new country with nothing. No house, no job, no money. We didn't know the laws, the language or the systems. Resources were scarce and the mounting pressure weighed heavily on my father. With two young children, a newborn baby and a wife to provide for in a new country, he had no other choice but to succeed. Determined, he took on a second job and then a third, and at home he was always angry. He had this anger building in him that none of us could explain. He would throw things, smash things, yell at us, and sometimes just stand there and scream. It wasn't long until he vented his anger at my mother, and then on us kids as well.

We now know he suffered terribly from post-traumatic stress disorder (PTSD). He would often wake up sweating and screaming from his nightmares of the war. Little was known about PTSD in those years, and so neither he nor his war veteran friends knew about the kinds of tools and the support that could help them to cope with this illness. He didn't know any better and soon passed on his anger to the next generation. As you can imagine, my brothers and I grew up in an environment full of fear, violence and abuse – along with huge expectations. My father was determined to raise four high achievers. He wanted to make sure that the sacrifices he and my mother made were honoured.

Determined to succeed, he quickly moved us to Bonnyrigg, close to the outer western suburb of Cabramatta in Sydney, NSW. It was during this time that he was bitten by the entrepreneurial bug, and he was bitten hard. He chose Cabramatta for its strong sense of community, and he saw how many of his friends had created a life for themselves there in a short period of time. He understood that the secret to their success was an unconditional dedication, often fuelled by an underlying desperation.

He found a prime business location in the heart of Cabramatta's bustling commercial district, and held this location for over ten years. On the first floor of the building, he operated a video library; downstairs, he ran a restaurant as well as an ice cream parlour. He also operated a driving school on the side. And my brothers and I provided the child labour. This is where my entrepreneurial journey began – at the tender age of seven.

Every morning before school, my father drove us all to the restaurant. My brothers' duty was to set up the tables and chairs inside and outside, while I helped my parents set up the kitchen. Once everything was ready, we caught the train to school and, after school, we caught the train back to the restaurant to help clean after lunch service and set up for dinner service. We then caught the bus home, where, every day, I cooked and cleaned for my brothers and made them do their homework and their household chores. This went on for years and years and years. I practically raised my brothers on my own while my parents worked and worked and worked. On top of all of this, we had to get good grades – or else a brutal caning ensued.

One thing was for certain: my father had created four tough working machines. He instilled into all of us a ferocious work ethic. I learned so much in those years. We all did. Mentally and physically we were strong. Emotionally and spiritually, however, we were a mess.

THE DREAM IS FREE; THE HUSTLE IS SOLD SEPARATELY

The positive side to all of this was that I quickly became self-sufficient. Mini entrepreneurial skills began to develop. Discipline, responsibility, accountability, reliability, persistency, courage, resilience and grit were some of my closest companions.

And soon, the hustler's spirit was born from these skills. Unbeknown to my parents, my brothers and I started operating a handsome business from home, selling packets of instant noodles to the Australian kids right from our front door. Each packet of instant noodles contained a sachet of artificial flavouring, packed full of monosodium glutamate (MSG – flavour enhancer 621), salt and tiny flakes of fake dry herbs. The Aussie kids would crush the crunchy uncooked noodles and sprinkle the fake flavouring on top. Then they would shake all the ingredients together and eat the contents straight out of the packet. Flavour. Bomb. They were addicted to MSG, and demanded that we keep supplying the goods.

In those days, the white kids were too scared to venture into Cabramatta (or 'Vietnam-matta', as it was known at the time) so we acted as their go-between. Each packet of instant noodles cost us 25 cents and we sold it on for $1. Every day after school, school kids from year three to year six lined up at our front door in Bonnyrigg, demanding their MSG fix. The explosion of new, unfamiliar flavours excited them. We thought the Aussie kids were crazy for wanting to pay this amount of money, but the demand was there – as was the profit margin – and so we thought, *Why the hell not?*

In later years, my youngest brother, Leroy (who is now a fashion designer), would also learn about supply and demand. He had two side hustles selling to his classmates in junior school. The first was selling the delicious fried peanuts that my father would make him for recess. The second was selling live fleas that he would pick from our flea-infested dogs. He trapped the parasites in clear plastic containers and sold them to the curious kids at school who had never before in their lives seen these tiny lively creatures. The jumping vermin provided a great deal of entertainment in the school yard.

We all knew that if our father ever found out about our little ventures, we would be in trouble big time. For sure he would beat us good and hard. Fear loomed over us as usual but we still found a way to run our rackets. Looking back, I cannot help but feel an incredible sense of pride about this. Despite our fear, we continued to take risks. We continued to be daring. We continued to work hard at the shop, continued to get good grades in school and continued to innovate with our side hustles. I had not yet turned ten years old.

FIGHTING FOR FREEDOM

The violence and abuse at home escalated during my teenage years. At school, the boys were starting to pay attention to me. As an awkward teenager with low self-esteem, it took me a long time to understand why. The anonymous love letters in my letter box and the generous gift hampers and teddy bears left at my front door were inevitably discovered by my father. I had no control over these love-sick deliveries, nor did I have control over the beatings that ensued. My father liked to humiliate me by cutting off my hair in chunks and lowering the hem of my school uniform to ankle length so that I could look as unattractive to the boys as possible.

By seventeen, I had had enough. I had become suicidal and severely depressed. I knew there had to be a better way. Every night, alone in my room, I would pray in the dark. 'Dear God, there has to be a better way than this. This can't be my life. This can't be my life.' And so, I mustered all the courage a teenage girl could muster and I ran away from home. I spent many years hiding from my father. I would look over my shoulder everywhere that I went, paranoid that familiar faces would follow me. I wanted my fears forgotten, not faced up to. I put myself through university and completed a Bachelor of Arts in Communications. By the time I was twenty, I was working two jobs to stay alive. I struggled to stay on top of the rent, bills and expenses from being at university and supporting myself.

Growing up in the family businesses helped me to get work quickly in some of the most prestigious restaurants in Sydney while I was at university. I scored positions working under the tutelage of famous chefs, restaurateurs and sommeliers. The ferocious work ethic that my father had instilled into me was quickly noticed by these respected professionals. I was often rewarded for being the hardest worker and achieving the highest sales results.

It was the early 90s and, while working in the best restaurants in Sydney, I came to know and observe many of the wealthy elite – businessmen, politicians, socialites and celebrities who didn't think twice about spending big on their corporate and personal credit cards to support their excesses and elevate their status. This was a new world for me. I had come from frugal beginnings. My life education came quickly with the help of my new-found friends. Sex, drugs, decadence and debauchery became my inner circle. Exposure to this fantasy world fuelled me. I was earning good money and spending it fast. I was hanging with the cool crowd who craved status, gluttony and control. I was influenced by the influencers and did not want this high life to end.

But every extreme high ends in a brutal comedown.

In my moments alone with these business icons and successful entrepreneurs – when we were naked, real and raw with each other – they would share with me their sadness, helplessness, frustration and longing. In these moments of honesty, incongruence and confusion set in. I had somehow wrongly made the assumption that if I acquired a fortune, I'd be home free – that all of my problems would be solved and I'd be catapulted into a rarefied existence where I'd be permanently happy. I didn't see anything like permanent happiness in the lives of these business icons and successful entrepreneurs, however.

All my life, I had watched my parents struggle. I'd watched them leave the house every morning before sunrise and return late at night, exhausted with aching bodies and deflated spirits. I'd watched them bicker and argue until their blood boiled to the point of explosion. And I'd watched them live cheerless lives while they reaped little financial reward. My parents had every right to be unhappy, but not these rich guys. They had no right to be unhappy. How could this be?

To be wealthy and unhappy didn't make any sense. This is not what success is meant to look like!

I decided then and there I wanted to find true success and true happiness – and so I went on a hunt to find it. The incongruence and confusion triggered me into a kind of life crisis. I was only twenty-two, so I guess it came earlier for me than most.

FYI – FOLLOW YOUR IRRITATION

And follow my irritation is exactly what I did. I left Australia and travelled the world. In my search, I travelled across Europe and lived many years in Paris and London. I spent time in the United States, Canada, the Caribbean, the Pacific Islands, Africa, Asia and India. I studied, trained and worked with some of the greatest spiritual teachers and entrepreneurs of our time. I met people in countries like China, Vietnam and India who were very poor materially but were spiritually very rich.

These experiences deepened my understanding that inner happiness and material wealth are not as intrinsically connected as I once thought. They are less like twin brothers who share the same bedroom and more like distant cousins who live on separate continents.

I wanted to find happiness for sure, but I also wanted to be wealthy. I did not want to experience the struggles that my parents and so many of their friends endured. My intuition told me that happiness and wealth were not actually a mutually exclusive proposition. My life experiences have proven to me that bringing them together is possible.

Being deeply spiritual and happy and fulfilled and materially wealthy can go hand in hand.

American writer Richard Bach put it perfectly when he said, 'You teach best what you most need to learn.' Over the years I have learned that the only way that I can continue to grow is to teach. My growth and fulfilment comes from my contribution to others. Zig Ziglar's words also ring true: 'You will get all you want in life if you help enough other people get what they want.' Over the years, I have learned that money doesn't buy you happiness; money buys you freedom and freedom is what buys you happiness. Happiness comes when we have the resources to assist others. Life is designed to make sure we express our unique talents and find fulfilment.

What we are destined to do as human beings is to find our talents and, through using our talents, benefit all humans. Our service to the world and what we are willing to receive for it come together to make up who we are. At the heart of this book is my desire to push forward humanity by teaching what many people still find a mystery today: that it can be success and happiness, not success or happiness. I call this the Way of the Spiritual Entrepreneur.

It is my mission to teach people how to master their hearts, their minds, their behaviours, their emotions and their environment so that they can live their lives fully and deliberately, and not by default. Mastering these areas is the key to entering the realm of the spiritual as well as material wealth and wellbeing.

This is true freedom.

HONOURING MY TEACHERS

If I have seen further, it is by standing upon the shoulders of giants. —Sir Isaac Newton

For as long as I can remember, I have been blessed with the unique knack of attracting great teachers. Even as a child, I was a magnet to the conscious educators. When my family first arrived in Australia as immigrants, my pre-school teacher, Ms Laurie Henley, took a liking to me and asked my father if I could live with her and her parents during the summer school holidays. I couldn't speak a word of English, but they always found a way to understand. The kindness, patience and generosity that she and her family showed me during those summer holidays will glow in my memory bank like a burning ember for as long as I live.

My journey to becoming a Spiritual Entrepreneur has continued to be fuelled by the assistance, advice, teachings, experiences, inspirations and love of many teachers, coaches and mentors. Many of whom are 'best in world' and have become my closest friends. I have never been afraid to seek wisdom from those who know more than me. Many mentors have told me that the secret is my speed. They find joy in teaching me because of my speed. They tell me, 'Pauline, the speed at which you learn is what improves your success. The urgency you apply to the execution is what makes you stand out. The speed of your actions and achievements is what gains our respect.'

Here's just a sample of how my teachers have helped my success:

- My writing coach taught me to 'write from the heart' and, without this, I would not have won the awards that I have won for my first book, *Secrets of the Red Lantern*. This international bestseller has changed the lives of many across the globe – not to mention my own.

- With the assistance of my speaking coach, I have become one of Australia's top keynote speakers. His guidance has given me the honour and privilege of now speaking and teaching on the world stage.

- The advice of my business mentors has seen our restaurant, Red Lantern (the most awarded Vietnamese restaurant in the world) win a multitude of business awards and entrepreneurial accolades over the decades. They have taught me time and time again that we can choose to be either iconic or mediocre – we can't be both.

- The teachings of my neurolinguistic programming (NLP) and developmental psychology coaches have allowed me to deeply understand human behaviour. And, as my coaches tell me, 'By understanding human beings, we can truly facilitate their highest expression.' It is because of their teachings that I now possess the skills to help transform many of my clients on their life journey – especially those who want to be much more high performing.

- My neuroscience coach continues to give me the insight that I need to understand how the human brain works. We must firstly understand ourselves, our beliefs and our limitations before we can positively assist others and effect sustainable change.

- Through the commitment of the personal trainers, yoga teachers, meditation gurus, movement coaches and martial art masters that I have had the privilege to work with across the globe, I have gained the flexibility of body, the strength of spirit and the agility of mind that disciplines, nurtures and sustains me today. It is an honour to pass on their teachings to my own students. They understand that if they are serious about business success, they cannot ignore the correlation between fitness and business excellence. Personal health, wellness and wellbeing are essential to bringing wealth and happiness to our business and our lives.

- The community of bio-hackers to which I belong continues to stimulate me with the tips and tools to elevate my body, my mind, my spirit and my environment. It is with this knowledge that I can assist my clients to upgrade their biology, smash their goals faster and level up their existence.

- The knowledge and kindness of my linguistic neural mentor has taught me to understand human interaction on a far deeper level. He is a master at the science and art of nonverbal communication. Without his expertise, I would not own the skills to positively affect and influence my audiences and students on any level, regardless of the group dynamic and classroom environment.

- Through the guidance of my science and spirituality teachers, and their astounding understanding of science, spirituality, humanity and the cosmos, I have been exposed to the understanding of the intelligence that expresses itself through the quantum laws of nature. My science and spirituality teachers have given me the courage to play a bigger game, encouraging me to share with more people the Way of The Spiritual Entrepreneur. Science is what demystifies the mystical. Science is what bridges cultures and unites us.

- And finally, my shamans have taught me a new way of being – of paying reverence to all that is, and of respecting the divine power of universal intelligence and the hidden order of all things. There is more to this reality than what is in the three-dimensional realm of the senses. Without the guidance of my shamans, I would not be blessed to experience oneness and wonder on a daily basis. This is where I have found true freedom.

Without a doubt, my teachers have fast-tracked my evolution. I would not be where I am today, as the woman I have become, if it were not for the wisdom that my teachers have bestowed upon me. They have made me look at my life and make better decisions to raise my standards. They push me to create new opportunities for myself to play a higher game of life.

SYNTHESISING THE WISDOMS

Please believe me when I tell you that if, in the past, you have experienced false prophets and fake motivators, you are not alone, and it is not your fault. I too made this mistake in the early years. My bad decisions have taught me to be excruciatingly discerning with those whose wisdom I choose to embody. Spiritual bankruptcy and incongruence is one of the greatest pandemics of our time – as is ego tripping, greed and deception. Reliance, dependency and quick fixes never work. The fastest way to disempower a society is to promote an impossible outcome.

The Way of the Spiritual Entrepreneur understands that we must build a solid foundation of self-realisation, self-understanding, self-acceptance and self-compassion before self-actualisation, self-determination, self-sustainability and self-transcendence can happen. Your teachers must have walked the walk! They must have experienced what it is like to sit in the discomfort of the fire. They must know how it feels to have fallen to their knees and risen from the ashes, like a Phoenix, to fly again and again and again. Your teachers must be living proof that it is possible.

The purpose of this book, as in my online programs and live events, is to provide you with the distinctions, understandings and tools that I have synthesised and developed over my lifetime. I have designed my programs especially for the entrepreneur – to further elevate and expand your mind, your heart, your health, your wealth, your brain, your body, your being and your spirit. In business and in life, your growth must be all-encompassing. No area can be ignored or neglected.

The network of Spiritual Entrepreneurs that I keep in my orbit hold me accountable and inspire me on a daily basis. They challenge me to rise higher and to continually grow into the next best version of myself so that I can teach more people on a global scale. They are quality human beings of high calibre. Together we push forward humanity with our ideas, our conversations and our associations. We do not waste valuable time with people who are not contributing to our growth. Our destiny is far too important.

I want this for you.

I want to show you that you CAN have it all.

Like my teachers before me, I too want to fast-track your evolution.

I too wish you godspeed on your journey as you reach for more, but remember this: if it does not bring you joy, it is not your truth.

Time and time again, I have made manifest my deepest heart's desire and thrived in the life I have always dreamed of because I have learned to travel this road with playfulness, with peacefulness, with inspiration, with friendship, with freedom, with love and with joy.

I want this for you.

Inner peace is my destination.

Joy is my GPS. Let it be your guide too as we get started.

KEY TERMS AND CONCEPTS

Before we get started on the main journey of the Spiritual Entrepreneur, making sure you understand some of the key terms and concepts that form the foundation of this book is worthwhile. Over the next few pages, I explain these ideas, starting with what I mean by spiritual, success and being an entrepreneur, before diving into the Way of the Spiritual Entrepreneur in more detail.

WHAT IS 'SPIRITUAL'?

Being spiritual means that we source our life from the divine. The term 'divine' could be defined as of or pertaining to a GOD. G.O.D – the grand organized design – to me is, the Universe, the intelligent expression of the synthesis and synchronicity of all that is. Divine means 'to shine', and that, as much as possible, we cultivate and express through our thoughts, words and actions the qualities of friendliness, love and compassion toward others. Being spiritual means that we incorporate our heart, our mind and our soul into our business and our spirit into our work. If we are in-spirit, we are inspired. The most fulfilled people I have ever met are the ones who are inspired. Spirituality opens our minds to a greater wisdom and truth and opens our hearts to a greater love and appreciation.

Spirituality, therefore, is a natural state of being.

Mike Dooley links in with these ideas, defining spirituality as:

> [T]he human recognition that there's more to reality than what the physical senses detect. It's the awareness of a supernatural

25

intelligence, of which you are a part. The awareness that there's order, meaning, and love behind all: that there's good everywhere, in everyone, and in everything. The awareness that you are eternal, powerful, resilient, and here to joyfully thrive.

Spiritual Entrepreneurship is not to be mistaken with the concept of 'spiritual materialism'. Many times, I have heard people get this wrong. Spiritual materialism revolves around self-delusion – that is, what some people believe is spiritual development is, in fact, strengthening their ego. Sometimes the delusion is subtle, like the arrogance that having encountered insight makes one better than other people. This is also known as the 'trap of superiority', which manifests as the tendency to look down upon others who are not as 'consciously advanced' or 'awakened'.

If the way we carry and express ourselves condemns others while lifting ourselves, we're as off-target as the people we're condemning. Inner silence and enviable peace don't come from the avoidance of life as it is; they come from moving as deeply into life as you can. The only way out is in and the only way beyond is through. No-one is better than anyone else. We all have different pit stops and destinations. Spiritual enlightenment is not about judgement or superiority. It is about surrender, authenticity, gratitude, and mindfulness. This includes being at peace with not only your own shadow, but also everyone else's. After all, it is the same shadow, simply cast upon a separate being.

Being spiritual also is not about being overtly spiritual. The first thing my shamans ever taught me was this: 'Do not get too spiritual – otherwise, you may lose the plot completely!'

They taught me that, as a spiritual leader with the power to teach and heal, it is easy to fall into the trap of ego and arrogance. Instead, they told me,

Stay grounded. Always be humble against your own limitations. Let your personality be your greatest work of art. Let go of your self-righteousness and habit of judging everything. Befriend your ego before you listen to the bullshit that tells you to destroy it.

Ego is what keeps you alive. Spirit is living life to the full. We need both to navigate this life.

To be spiritual is to possess a transcendent mind. Transcendence will set you free.

The transcendental mind sees both sides of an event. This allows for absolute presence. The imminent mind only sees one side without the other. The speed at which you can see both sides of an event means you are operating at a higher frequency and have chosen enlightenment over endarkenment. The practice is to use this energy to transcend your limitations, and to channel abundance and courage. When you ascend into a higher dimensional field, you will never think the same way again. There is no turning back. You cannot un-know what you now know.

To be spiritual is to be connected to all that is. This is the understanding that the influence we have over our existence is directly linked to the connection between all things, as all things and particles are entangled. When this becomes your reality, you will never be lonely.

Spiritual Entrepreneurs understand that we can manifest our own reality. Our realities are so fluid that they can change in a second without thought. Your reality reflects what dimension you experience. (More on this, and how it connects to the quantum field of intelligence, in the later chapters of this book.)

At its core, the Way of the Spiritual Entrepreneur is the process of self-realisation which, in itself, is a deeply spiritual process. It is about getting really aware of yourself and where you really are. Behind the 'self' is who you really are, which is the true expression of your Unis – your Universe. It is not who you take yourself to be, but who you are in this moment, at your very, very best, expressing yourself now, and not from the bondage of past structures. Spirituality is not about being in some higher realm, but the true expression of YOU. With self-realisation comes freedom. Freedom from 'self' will give you clarity. You will become calmer and more responsive in the world, rather than being a 'reactive' self.

Before we can begin to understand others, we must first interrogate and understand ourselves. When we can deeply know, accept and influence ourselves, we can then master the art of influence over others and be of greater service to our families and our communities at home and on a global scale.

To know thyself is to thyself be true.

In a world that reveres superficiality, we go deep.

WHAT IS SUCCESS VERSUS SPIRITUAL SUCCESS?

Throughout my childhood years, my parents as well as my uncles and aunties would indoctrinate me with their meaning of success. 'Get good grades at school. Excel in science and mathematics and you will be successful with everything in life. Go to university. Study law or medicine and you will be successful with everything in life. Become a doctor or lawyer. Get married to a doctor or lawyer. Buy a big house. Have children. Get your children to make you grandchildren. Look after your parents when they get old. Retire. Die.'

I believed all of this as truth until I ran away from home at the age of seventeen and realised that I wanted none of it. The strongest motivation that fuelled me was that I did not want to be like everyone else. It simply wasn't in my DNA.

I knew there must be more to life than what my family had indoctrinated me with – and, indeed, there was more! The party scene combined with the hospitality scene gave me a taste of the high life and opened doors for me to play with some major influencers. My crew knew all the important maître d' from the finer restaurants and we made friends with the important bouncers and 'door bitches' who, in turn, introduced us to other important people in their VIP establishments. This particular crowd was always warm and welcoming.

At the nightclubs and private parties, one man showed up often in my periphery. He was shy and flamboyant at the same time. He made eye contact when he saw me and would nod acknowledgement, but never introduced himself. From top to toe, he donned mismatched designer wear – Prada, Louis Vuitton and Gucci were his preferred choices. Despite the expensive threads, he still managed to look like a bum. He liked to surround himself with a gaggle of pretty young Asian girls. They made him look important and they felt important being around him.

Meet wealthy 'TJ'

My friends finally told me about this man. 'Oh yes, TJ,' they said. 'He's one of the wealthiest property developers in town. He went to Sydney Grammar and comes from a rich family. He took over the family business and has done well for himself. The man is smart. Incredibly intelligent. He's been able to grow his family business by expanding from waterfront development to hotel development. His net worth is more than $120 million dollars.'

Through these influencers, TJ and I became friends. The first time he invited me into his home, he gave what was clearly a well-rehearsed tour of his waterfront mansion. He showed off his underground garage, housing a McLaren, a Ferrari, a Lamborghini, a Bentley and a Maserati. His eyes beamed as he pulled out his shiny watch collection from the showcase cabinet in the front room. He told me they were the most expensive watches in the world – Perrelet, Patek Philippe, IWC Portugieser, D'Audemars Piguet. I almost choked on the vintage Dom when he told me that he paid $85,000 for one of the watches. I don't know what impressed him the least – the fact that I had never heard of these brands, or that I asked him why he needed so many watches.

TJ told me that whenever he travelled, he flew only first class; that, when he dined out, which was almost every night, the bill was never less than $1000. This excess showed up clearly in his physicality. He was inflamed, lethargic, bloated and overweight. When we dined out together, it was always in a group and the dining companions would order excessively. They cared very little about wastage or sustainability. 'What for? TJ will cover the bill.' I came from frugal beginnings – the waste of food as well as the mindless eating and drinking made me incredibly uncomfortable.

TJ could never hold a long-term relationship. A different girl hung on his arm every couple of months. TJ partied every weekend and I watched as his health deteriorated. He could barely walk up the stairs without running out of breath. He often complained about how much sleep he didn't have. His doctor put him on a sleep apnoea machine to help with the unbearable insomnia that he suffered. And each New Year's Eve, he held 'the party of the year' at his waterfront mansion, and the sycophants came in droves. They came, ate his food, drank his alcohol, took the essential selfie on his balcony with the stunning view in the background, and then they left.

Although he had a large network of friends, he told me in private how lonely he was. That he moved through girls so quickly because he got bored of them easily. TJ also told me he was deeply depressed. He had absolutely everything I could ever imagine anyone wanting or needing to be permanently happy and yet he was depressed. While he never showed it in public, he would often complain to me about his vacuous friends, his gold-digger girlfriends and the looming pressures of his work. All his life, he had worked hard to gain respect and acceptance from others through his material acquisitions. Indeed, he had created a massive network of friends and acquaintances and invested in a vast collection of material possessions, but still he remained depressed and unfulfilled.

I am still unsure why TJ confided in me so much. Clearly his other friendships didn't have a lot of substance, but we weren't best mates either. Perhaps it was because I was a power listener, saying very little when he told me about his life. Perhaps it was because I never wanted anything from him. Perhaps it was because he knew that I found him fascinating. The one word that popped into my head the most whenever I saw TJ was incongruence.

American psychologist Carl Rogers introduced the concept of incongruence to psychology in the 1950s. He defined congruence as the matching of experience and awareness. Incongruence was, therefore, lacking congruence, or having feelings not aligned with your actions.

Like so many of his friends, TJ was spiritually bankrupt. He couldn't understand the concept of being 'fully present in the moment', and found it hard to maintain focus in conversations – even with loved ones. He lived in an exquisite mansion overlooking Sydney's breath-taking harbour, but couldn't find joy in the simple pleasures of appreciating the sunrise or savouring the sunset. He had the resources to eat the healthiest foods and hire the best personal trainer money could buy, but his meaning of success was so warped that the incongruence grew inside him like a cancer.

The concept of spirit and spirituality might seem abstract or cliché to some, but I know first-hand how illness can manifest in the face of a broken spirit. It was clear that TJ was overcompensating for something. Like so many, TJ was unhappy because he was not in alignment with who he was – not because of what anyone else was doing.

I have no doubt that, as a young man, TJ overflowed with an authentic spirit. He wouldn't have strived to achieve his material wealth and portfolio had he not. But somewhere along the way, he lost it. Even with a fortune in excess of $120 million, his people still laughed at him behind his back. He strived to become worthy, to meet other people's standards, to check off all the boxes of what was supposed to make him happy according to other people's ideals – the big houses, the jobs, the cars, the watches, the clothes, the girls, the network, the net worth – only to realise that he was empty and incomplete.

While this traditional definition of success – that is, making vast sums of money and acquiring beautiful houses, cars and boats – is not wrong, it is only defining the gross surface layer of success. True spiritual success cannot be defined exclusively in material terms. It is surely not success if you are wealthy but unhealthy, or wealthy but the people around you don't like you or only pretend to like you, or if you are wealthy but feel unhappy.

Yes, it is important to be committed to your business and financial goals; however, we need to recalibrate the definition of the word 'success' to be broader and more encompassing, including our spirit, if we are to live our life's potential.

WHAT IS AN ENTREPRENEUR?

Entrepreneurs are innovative, daring, creative and ambitious self-starters. The word entrepreneur is a French word that literally means, 'one who undertakes (some task)'. But the English meaning of the word has developed over time, with Dictionary.com defining it as 'a person who organizes and manages any enterprise, especially a business, usually with considerable initiative and risk'. Entrepreneurs, in the purest sense, are those who identify a need – any need – and fill it. This is a primordial urge, independent of product, service, industry or market.

There is a common pattern that occurs in the childhood lives of entrepreneurs. Most entrepreneurs have been challenged by their fathers as youths – whether this challenge has been to get off their arse and go to work and be accountable, or to go out into the world and fend for themselves, or something harsher altogether. If you have been challenged, or felt like you have been challenged, the common outcome is that you accelerate, you generate, you grow and you lead. On the other hand, when the mother has overprotected you and you have received more support in your childhood than challenges, you slow down your development – whether this is in the womb, after the womb or at any stage, it still applies – you decelerate and degenerate and become a follower. Entrepreneurs are people who seek more challenges, while intrapreneurs are people who seek more support from other people.

Typically, entrepreneurs are motivated in three ways. The first two are fairly common but limit us to financial success only and, in most cases, leave the person rich but disillusioned – which to them still feels like failure.

The third way, is the road less travelled, and is the Way of the Spiritual Entrepreneur.

First let's look at the three ways entrepreneurs are motivated to succeed:

1. *Through fear of pain:* Entrepreneurs focused on this motivation ask questions like, 'What will happen to me if I don't achieve my goals? I don't want to end up on the street, cold, hungry and lonely.' When you are trying to avoid pain, you are motivated

by the idea of moving away from what you don't want to have happen. Where your focus goes, your energy flows. The more you focus on avoiding pain, the more you will attract it. It is impossible to be happy if you are stuck in this mindset.

2. *Through an inner sense of lack:* This type of drive to succeed can be thought of as a kind of inner wound, and can originate from a rough childhood with parents who found it difficult to be nurturing, or a family environment with limited resources, or from consistently being berated and belittled as a child. It is amazing how far a person can go when being driven by the idea of, 'I'm going to be successful just so I can prove [fill in the blank] that I can achieve', or 'I'm going to be successful so I never have to go without [fill in the blank]'. With this outlook, being wealthy is indeed possible, but being truly happy is not. Sadly, this wound is never healed or overcome by any amount of financial success or recognition.

3. *Through an inspiring mission:* This is a dream of the world becoming a better place as a result of the proliferation of your product or service. When you are on purpose, with a mission, you are driven by the thought of 'moving toward' something that you consider your life's calling. Motivated in this way, the entrepreneur is both inspired and fulfilled and has a tremendous shot at being extremely wealthy.

COMBINING SPIRITUALITY AND WEALTH: THE WAY OF THE SPIRITUAL ENTREPRENEUR

Spiritual and material are often thought of as two completely separate entities. When I spoke to a friend about this book having the title *The Way of the Spiritual Entrepreneur*, they said, 'That's an oxymoron if ever I've heard one!' In doing so, they echoed the prevailing worldview, that the spiritual and material dimensions of life are separate. Deep in the mainstream psyche exists the idea that we cannot be wealthy and spiritual at the same time.

Everything is spirit, and material things are all the more so because so much imagination, love, effort and energy has gone into thinking about them, creating them, acquiring them and sharing them. I would like you to think of the spiritual and the material as one thing. Imagine a continuum where, to the left, we have the spiritual and, to the far right, we have the material. The material is the stuff we can taste, touch, feel and detect with our five senses. Houses, cars, boats and planes are a few examples.

The spiritual is to do with the realm of reality that is subtle and invisible. Thoughts, ideas, intuition and emotions such as joy, peace and happiness are some examples. We could say that the material is the gross or dense layer of reality and the spiritual is the layer that is subtle. Spirit requires matter to express itself and matter needs spirit to give it motion and meaning.

The main thing to remember is the material and the spiritual are one thing. Opposite ends of the one spectrum but connected. There is no existence without a perfect unity of the two. If we overlook this fact, we can be brainwashed into the notion that we can't be wealthy, spiritual and happy simultaneously.

We could even fall prey to the idea that there is nobility in poverty and that being spiritual means we should own very little and being wealthy means we are dishonest or taking advantage of others.

Scarcity and poverty mindsets repel opportunity and hold us back from living our dream life and manifesting our deepest desires. We are not born to barely get by, pay our bills and die. We are here to create and recreate the next best versions of ourselves and experience our lives with richness, abundance and joy.

Ideas such as 'they are filthy rich' or 'money is the root of all evil' communicate that prevailing worldview that being wealthy is somehow perverse. The notion that people with money aren't spiritual is simply not a rule. Nothing could be further from the truth. Scarcity and poverty is what keeps people powerless and in a state of suffering.

It is possible to be deeply spiritual, incredibly happy and wealthy at the same time. Indeed, to be poor and unhappy is no fun, and to be wealthy and unhappy is also missing the point. To be happy and materially poor is admirable, but to be happy and wealthy is enviable. If we have awareness that the spiritual and material layers of life are one thing, we can go about the business of having an extraordinary life. Then we will have the ability to be extremely happy and wealthy simultaneously. Spiritual wealth and material wealth are two of the greatest motivating forces in the human psyche. When these two forces come together, an incredible power is unleashed.

On my journey, I have met:

1. poor and unhappy people

2. poor and happy people

3. wealthy and unhappy people

4. wealthy and happy people.

The final type of people – those who have it all and are wealthy and happy – are extremely rare.

This split of where people can sit in the combination of happiness and wealth can also be seen in the following figure. The purpose of this book is to help you get to Quadrant 4, the realm of the Spiritual Entrepreneur.

The Happiness-Wealthy Quadrant

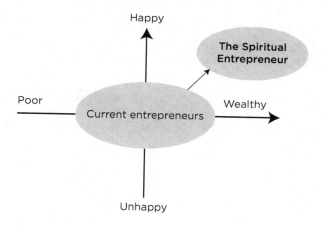

I have worked with many, many entrepreneurs. One of the most impressive was Dr Olivia Dam, medical director, cataract surgeon and owner of Victoria Eye in British Columbia, Canada, where she lived with her husband and two children.

When I first met Olivia, we were at A-Fest in Mykonos, Greece. Amid the learnings and festivities, she shared with me her dream of working in impoverished countries to restore sight to those incapacitated by blindness.

She wanted to transform their lives so that they could become functional and productive again. Olivia ranked extremely high on the wealth continuum, and was also very happy. The question for Dr Olivia wasn't how to move from poor to wealthy or from unhappy to happy, because she was already both. The question was how high to move her into the far top right corner of Quadrant 4. With the good doctor, it was all about fine-tuning, and some of the tools I offered Olivia privately are the same ones I offer in my live event, Awaken the Spiritual Entrepreneur.

The ideas and tools in Awaken the Spiritual Entrepreneur are not taught as a way to detach, but as a new way of life for entrepreneurs. It is my single-minded mission to show people what can be accomplished when we cross the traditional boundaries between science and spirituality.

I am obsessed with showing that we are much more than just our linear minds. The Way of the Spiritual Entrepreneur removes the limitations of the present and reclaims the multidimensional life that we were born to lead by underpinning deceptively simple practices with hard science. By marrying state-of-the-art discoveries of biology, genetics and behavioural science with ancient wisdom, we gain a powerful framework for understanding what is possible in our lives.

Spiritual success is the progressive realisation of a worthy ideal.

Spiritual success is having your work be meaningful – because meaning is what brings the real richness to your life. Spiritual success is creating a phenomenal lifestyle and living your life in a way that causes you to feel abundant pleasure and very little pain. What you really want to strive to do is to be surrounded by people you trust and treasure, having a network of friends who cherish you and elevate you. That's when you are living in Quadrant 4 and are really rich – happy and wealthy. This is true spiritual success.

People are sold on the idea that success equals happiness. The spiritual is often ignored, because society places so much emphasis on material success alone, but as I've discussed, success isn't just about making money and climbing the social ladder. Sure, money matters; but having a lot of money does not automatically make you a truly successful person. Certain freedoms only come through having money. What you want is to have money that adds meaning to your life. Happiness is an emotion; it ultimately fades away, just as all emotions do. Feelings of pleasure are fleeting. Meaning on the other hand is enduring.

For example, is it not deeply spiritual to have raised $50 million each year to help children in developing countries get the education they deserve? Isn't this pushing forward humanity? Or to create a business that employs people and contributes to supporting their families while creating wealth for your own children and their children's children. Isn't this sharing the wealth and pushing humanity forward? What if you used this money to take your kids on international adventures, giving them an expansive world view and creating citizens of the universe? Isn't this spreading the love and pushing humanity forward? What if you donated $5 million to scientific research to find cures for deadly diseases? Or gave to a charity that fights famine in underdeveloped countries? Success is using your life to make a massive impact. It's time to quash the notion that material wealth is somehow not spiritual.

The competitive edge

The greatest Spiritual Entrepreneurs have the competitive edge and the unfair advantage. They are trained to remain calm and focused, to live in the present, and to embrace and explore the beauty of their creations. The greatest Spiritual Entrepreneurs challenge the illusions of fear, lies, false beliefs and judgements that create suffering and unhappiness in their lives.

The greatest Spiritual Entrepreneurs understand that it is a war that takes place in the heart and the mind. He or she is trained to face this challenge with the clarity and awareness that this war is fought within themselves and that truth and unconditional love are on the other side of these battles. You see, Spiritual Entrepreneurs are engaged, connected, and fulfilled. They understand that the ultimate quest is the quest for calm courage and personal freedom.

SO HOW DO YOU BECOME A SPIRITUAL ENTREPRENEUR?

This book is all about getting you into Quadrant 4, the realm of the Spiritual Entrepreneur, and I have broken the journey down for you. The following chapters outline the seven guaranteed secrets to achieving this status and becoming fearless, stress free, and unshakable, and you will see how this gives the Spiritual Entrepreneur the competitive edge and the unfair advantage in business and in life.

In each of the chapters ahead I provide steps and tools so you can begin the practices right away. Remember the words of my teachers. The speed at which you learn is what improves your success. The urgency you apply to the execution is what will make you stand out. The speed of your actions and achievements is what will gain the respect, love and admiration of those around you – but, more importantly, that of yourself.

Many have implemented these seven secrets, but if you really want to fast-track your evolution, and embody the Way of The Spiritual Entrepreneur for the rest of your life, you can also attend my Awaken the Spiritual Entrepreneur retreat, and gain the full support of our community.

So, let us begin.

'The Way' Secret #1

REDEFINING HAPPINESS

The Master in the art of living makes little distinction between his work and his play, his labour and his leisure, his mind and his body, his information and his recreation, his love and his religion. He hardly knows which is which.

He simply pursues his vision of excellence at whatever he does, leaving others to decide whether he is working or playing. To him he's always doing both.

—James A. Michener

The first step to moving towards the utopia of Quadrant 4 is understanding lasting happiness. To do this, we must first redefine what it means to be happy.

I WILL BE HAPPY WHEN ...

Most of us fail at working out what happiness means, and instead fall into the trap of thinking, *I will be happy when my spouse changes his/her behaviour.* Or *I will be happy when the client gives me this big account.* Or *I will be happy when I lose 15 kg.* Or *I will be happy when I finally marry the man of my dreams.* Or *I will be happy when I can afford to buy that fancy car.* Or *I will be happy when my children finally do as I say.* Or *I will be happy when I am financially free.*

It is clear that happiness for the entrepreneur occurs most when they are adding value to people's lives. Entrepreneurs own businesses or organisations that solve other people's problems, they move resources from areas of low productivity to areas of high productivity, offering additional benefits to their customers and clients – whether that be in areas of health, wealth or relationships – and receiving money in return. In the effort to serve and please everybody else, however, entrepreneurs too often forget about themselves.

The Spiritual Entrepreneur, on the other hand, works first on increasing their baseline level of happiness, so that they can have a big picture view on life. They crystallise their personal priorities consciously, so that they can get good at life. This is what matters the most. The Spiritual Entrepreneur pays attention to their mental and emotional form as well as their health, heart and soul. The Spiritual Entrepreneur understands that they have but one glorious life, and it is their duty to master all areas of its magnificence.

Happiness and fulfilment for the Spiritual Entrepreneur comes from the consistent mastery of their life, and its continued evolution. This is how they can be of the greatest service to themselves, their family, their businesses and community at home and on a global scale.

We are naturally happier when we design our life consciously.

Let me repeat that.

We are naturally happier when we design our life consciously.

I learned this valuable lesson the hard way.

In 2018 our restaurant, Red Lantern, turned sixteen years old, placing us in the top 4 per cent of businesses in the world – those that have survived more than ten years in business. Red Lantern is the most awarded Vietnamese restaurant in the world. Today, under the umbrella of Red Lantern, my brother Luke, my husband, Mark, and I travel the world, make television, write, speak around the globe, coach, mentor and teach.

With a string of travel shows and cookbooks under his belt, Luke is now one of the most syndicated chefs in the world, with restaurants in multiple countries as well as tenures overseeing the menu for first and business class on Etihad and Vietnam Airlines. Mark is also a celebrated chef who is well known for his commitment to sustainability and the ethics of what we eat – a topic Red Lantern is most passionate about. Our lives today, while not without their challenges, are rewarding, eventful, inspiring and fun.

But it hasn't always been this way. Far from it.

Red Lantern opened in 2002, and we opened with a bang. We were fully booked every night and the waitlist was long. This was a great problem to have, but it was a problem nevertheless. You see, we all knew how to work hard. We didn't know how to work hard *and* work smart. We worked eighty-, ninety-, sometimes one-hundred-hour weeks. Week after week after week. We were stressed. We were tired all the time. We had no life.

Luke's dreams of entertaining his friends at the front of house never happened because he was stuck in the kitchen all the time. Mark's dreams of riding his Ducati and fly fishing on his days off never happened because he never had days off. And my dreams of having children were still dreams because Mark and I were simply too tired after work to do anything else but sleep. Things got so bad that I developed alopecia – a condition that causes the hair to fall out due to stress.

In the first month of operation, Red Lantern won Best New Restaurant and Best Asian Restaurant (a rank we held for four years in a row), and the awards kept coming. The waitlists grew and the intensity of the first few years strained us. Sometimes the phones rang so hot, the entire system crashed. One night, after a long and difficult service, the three of us sat down for our after-work beer. It was 2 am, as usual. My body ached. My back and shoulder muscles burned from carrying and clearing hundreds of plates each day. The nerves on the side of my neck pinched and twanged like wires on a harp. The sciatica pain in the side of my legs shot all the way down to the bottom of my feet – the result of hours treading the floorboards balancing stacks of heavy plates in each hand. It was always at the end of the night, when we finally stopped, that the throbbing would amplify. Sometimes the pain was so acute, I could barely breathe.

We were tired. We were tired of being tired. That morning, at 2 am, we looked at each other and we cried. 'What are we doing?' I asked. 'Look at us! We look terrible. We've all lost so much weight. We're miserable. We have no life. I've lost all my freaking hair!' And it was in this moment that I had flashbacks of my parents working like dogs to the point of exhaustion every day throughout my childhood, and it fascinated (and scared) me how history has a way of repeating.

This wasn't the reason we went into business!

We went into business to have fun, to learn, to grow, to contribute, to have a life, to leave a legacy! Yes, we were making money and winning awards and making a name for ourselves, but the truth was, none of us could say that we were happy. In fact, most days, we were down-right miserable. Like many of our entrepreneur friends, we'd possessed the warped view that we would be happy when we received the fame, the glory and the fortune. We thought we would be happy when all the awards were on the wall and we could walk around with big smiles on our faces. We lived our lives as if all was well. But our smiles were fake and we didn't know it. We were pretending and we didn't know it. We were still asleep and we didn't know it.

We were miserable because we had our priorities all wrong.

We were miserable because we were not in alignment with who we truly were.

We were miserable because we couldn't see the big picture.

SEEING THE BIG PICTURE

You cannot have lasting happiness until you can see the big picture. If you cannot see the big picture, you will get blindsided by the things you don't see coming around the corner. Stress, anxiety, overwhelm, fear and sickness can easily creep up and consume you when you are caught unaware.

Take the two frogs in a well. One is at the bottom of the well, the other at the top. The frog at the bottom of the well thinks that the circle of sky he is seeing is in fact the whole sky. The frog at the top of the well sees the entire sky.

Sometimes we can go through life like the frog at the bottom of the well – we think we see the big picture and that is all there is to our world. But there is so much more we are not seeing. It is impossible to see the big picture from where we are currently standing. When we can change our position in life, when we can ascend, when we can change our world view, our lives instantly fill with awe and wonder. When we can see the big picture, we can anticipate the future and respond to life's demands with fearlessness, grace and poise. Our world becomes expansive and we experience how miraculous our life truly is.

Remember – we do not climb mountains so that people can see us; we climb mountains so that we can see the world.

Let me put things into perspective with the big picture view.

We live on a planet in the middle of a Universe that is so incredibly vast that scientists cannot fathom its magnitude. It is time, not space that limits our view of the Universe. Beyond a certain distance, light hasn't had time to reach us yet. The Universe continues to expand faster than our mind and our heart can ever know. It is impossible to know how much more there is out there.

In 2003, NASA photographed the oldest picture of the Universe. It has taken the light from that point nearly 14 billion years to reach us. Keep in mind that light travels at 300,000 km a second. So, if you could travel 300,000 km every second for 14 billion years you would reach the outer edges of the known Universe. That distance is likely beyond comprehension, so consider this – if you could travel at the speed of light, you could travel around the earth 7.5 times in one second. Amazing, right?

Scientists estimate that five times more stars are in our Universe than there are grains of sand on every beach on the planet, and yet Alpha Centauri, the closest star system to our Solar System, is located a short 4.24 light-years away from our Sun. So, it would take four and a quarter years travelling at 300,000 km a second to get there. The distances are so vast it is mind-boggling. Compared to the size of the Universe, our little planet is insignificant. What does that say about a human life?

Carl Sagan sums it up:

> *Look again at that dot, that's here, that's home, that's us. On it everyone you love, everyone you know, everyone you ever heard of, every human being who ever was, lived out their lives. The aggregate of our joy and suffering, thousands of confident religions, ideologies, and economic doctrines, every hunter and forager, every hero and coward, every creator and destroyer of civilization, every king and peasant, every young couple in love, every mother and father, hopeful child, inventor and explorer, every teacher of morals, every corrupt politician, every 'superstar', every 'supreme leader', every saint and sinner in the history of our species lived there – on a mote of dust suspended in a sunbeam.*

You might be thinking, *Where are you going with all of this, Pauline?* Bear with me for a little longer.

Planet Earth is 4.5 billion years old. Our species, the Homo sapiens, are believed to have emerged almost 200,000 years ago. Each human being is made up of 70 to 100 trillion cells, and each one of those cells is made up of 100 trillion atoms. If you were to enlarge these atoms to the size of a baseball, approximately two football fields of empty space would be between those atoms. That is how much space is in and around you, existing as potential energy.

Now, let's consider time in reference to our own lives. The average life expectancy of a human being in the world's most affluent countries is roughly 82 years old. But let's suppose we take good care of ourselves and exceed the average. Let's imagine we are lucky enough to live for 100 years. (And, indeed, modern science and medical advancements sees this rapidly becoming the norm.) If we live for 100 years we get 36,500 days on the planet.

Significant issues need to be considered here. Longevity is of prime importance.

If you live to 100, how will you design your quality of life? How will you design your quality of character? Will you choose to live your life deliberately or by default? Will you live out your days filled with a sense of purpose, a sense of joy, love and adventure? Or will you be trapped by the same old routines and expired skill sets?

Will you actualise your true potential or will you remain caged, comfortable and stale? Will you engage in new and challenging activities or will you go on cruise control for years and autopilot your way through the opportunities life throws at you? Will you continue to create, collaborate and innovate, and make your mark on this world, or will you be proud of your mediocrity?

Will you be strong, fit, healthy and vital to help solve people's problems for the rest of your life, or will you deteriorate slowly and become a burden to your family and to society? Will you be in optimum state to do your best work and be of use to serve humanity better, or will you continue sleepwalking for the rest of your days? How will you leave a legacy that lasts forever?

Yes, we will live longer, but the reality is, when you look at the big picture, we still don't get much time in the overall scheme of things.

Where I am going is here: if we don't see the big picture, we can ignore the fact that our life as a human on this little planet is finite.

We can live in ignorance, with a false sense that we are never going to die. Seeing the big picture is both mind-blowing and awe inspiring. It most certainly helps us put our life in perspective – starting with not sweating the small stuff. When we see the big picture, we are ignited to live a charged life – a truly lived life. Ralph Waldo Emerson puts it beautifully: 'We are always getting ready to live but never living.' Just because we are alive, it doesn't mean we are living.

EMBRACING MORTALITY

It is normal to get a little depressed when we think about our mortality, but if we can always see the big picture and the time we have left on this earth, it becomes liberating.

Here are five reasons:

1. We start listening to our heart more. If we ignore our inevitable fate, we can fall into the trap of ignoring our hearts calling and postponing what we are hungry to do with our life. At the end of our days, we don't want to be thinking, *Oh my God, I wish I had gone on that sailing trip* – or climbed that mountain, or told that person we loved them, or had children, or created that business, or gone on that adventure, or the myriad of other regrets.

2. We begin to view our time as a precious resource. We reclaim our agenda. We evaluate in the most informed way our priorities, and what we are doing with our life. As a result, better decisions are made about how we spend our time and who we spend our time with. We begin to design our life consciously.

3. As we recognise that time is precious, we stop delaying. We offer life our very best and we make an effort to thoroughly enjoy and appreciate each precious moment.

4. We become free of petty habits like envy, judgement and making comparisons to others. We naturally start to cultivate qualities of compassion and friendliness because we can see that we are all in the same boat, and everyone on this planet is a part of the journey.

5. We give up attempting to control everything, because we comprehend that so much of what happens in life is beyond our personal control. A hidden order is at play. This means we can let go and relax and enjoy life a lot more.

> *The spiritual journey is individual, highly personal. It can't be organised or regulated. It isn't true that everyone should follow one path. Listen to our own truth. We're all just walking each other home.* —Ram Dass

So that morning, at 2 am, in the middle of the Red Lantern dining room, I took the first step. I admitted to myself the painful truth – that, despite the success and accolades, my life was, in fact, joyless. I didn't want it this way anymore. I wanted excitement. I wanted fulfilment. I wanted adventure. I wanted to grow. I wanted to contribute. I wanted to push humanity forward in some way. I wanted to make my mark on this world. I knew deep in my heart that there was more I could be.

I wanted to give life to life.

And it was in that moment of decision that my destiny was shaped. There was, however, one catch: I understood that before I could master a new way of being, I had to master a new way of thinking.

As Dr Joe Dispenza puts it, 'You cannot change your personal reality, unless you change your personality.' And the law of attraction ideas teach that:

> *What you think you will become. What you feel you will attract. What you imagine you will create. The happiness of your life depends upon the quality of your thoughts. The greatest secret of mankind is that you can change your life by altering the images in your mind. What you are afraid to do is a clear indication of the next thing you need to do.*

Until I faced my deepest fear and changed myself first, I knew I could never succeed. I had to literally become a new person. This was the scariest part. But on that morning, Mark, Luke and I vowed to one another that we would do things differently. We vowed to one another that we wouldn't stop working hard – instead, we would work hard and work smart. We vowed to one another that we would rewrite our story and redesign our destiny, and continue to reinvent ourselves. We vowed to one another that from this point forth, we would live our lives deliberately and not by default. But in order to do this, we had to rethink the nexus of being on the tools or leading from the front. We had to find a way to climb out of the quagmire that we had trapped ourselves in.

Because we knew no fate determines our future. We determine our future.

One life on this earth is all that we get, whether it is enough or not enough, and the obvious conclusion would seem to be that at the very least we are fools if we do not live it as fully and bravely and beautifully as we can. —Frederick Buechner

THE PAIN OF REGRET

In early 2000, after the death of my grandmother, my brother Lewis and I were consumed by the guilt, frustration and sorrow of her long and drawn out decline. We wanted to confront our own fears around death and dying.

We volunteered our time at a hospice in downtown London. The old and the dying do not get visitors often, and so isolation and loneliness haunt them in their final days. We visited the hospice weekly and had the chance to get to know people who only had a short time to live – most only a few weeks. We learned so much during this time. A hospice is the place where the sick go to die – when the doctors have exhausted all hope of saving them. In hospice patients, there is no more fighting to survive. There is only surrender. Because of this, the place is stripped of pretence and facade. It is a place free of egocentric behaviour. Transparency and honesty prevails.

Lewis is livelier than I am. He is the kindest, most generous and most upbeat man I know. He also loves to cook, and so the hospice manager allowed us to visit every Friday from 2 pm to 4 pm to perform cooking demonstrations. Lewis was able to get many of the residents involved in the preparation and cooking, and we all ate together afterwards. Lewis has a knack of making people laugh, injecting the room with pure energy everywhere that he goes. When Lewis is 'on', he is 'on'! I, on the other hand, preferred to sit quietly in the corner, observing, journalling, taking it all in, watching my brother in action and assisting silently.

What touched us the most was seeing how much the residents came out of their shells during our visits. We realised the most poignant room in the hospice was the kitchen, which was indeed a revelation considering that most of the residents could eat very little, if anything at all. The first time Lewis cooked spring rolls, the old residents, who usually sat in their wheelchairs and stared at the wall or ceiling, actually participated in the rolling of the spring rolls. It was a delight providing sustenance for the residents on many levels, including their sense of smell, taste, touch and play – primal sensorial delights. Lewis and I tended to the dignity of the senses by way of the body – impulses that helped them stay present. Even if only for a short period of time, they didn't think about their past or their future. We learned that, as long as we have our senses, even just one, we have at least the possibility of accessing what makes us feel human and connected.

We also learned that, no matter how old we get, we all crave human connection – to feel like we are a part of something. And we learned that as we get older, we do not lose our innate characteristics such as competitiveness, humour and grace. It made Lewis happy when the staff told him how much the residents were looking forward to his visits. The staff also admitted that his visits added laughter to their usual sombre routines. His visits were the times when the most number of staff turned up to work. When the residents were wrapping spring rolls, they made fun of each other's rolling skills and tried to beat each other, to roll faster than the other. Lewis and I would steal secret glances at each other and giggle because the residents were really old but still so competitive and wanted to win. It made us sad knowing that they didn't have many magic moments left to share laughter and joy with one another.

I remember Mary and Kate in particular. Mary was in the final stages of Alzheimer's, and her best friend Kate was dying of cancer. Even though they were frail and weak, they were both excited to wrap the spring rolls. Mary and Kate were an absolute pleasure to be around. Their animated excitement at wrapping the spring rolls gave me glimpses of how playful and cheeky they must have been in their youth. Kate was incredibly slow but incredibly determined. With their shaky hands, they made the morsels look more like pasties than spring rolls. Mary teased Kate endlessly and gave her so much grief for being slow. I cried silent tears of happiness watching the two of them laughing and giggling together like two young girls getting up to mischief. One Friday afternoon, Mary told us that Kate was too weak to attend the cooking demonstration. On the following Friday afternoon, the staff told us that both ladies had passed away.

Sometimes the staff, as well as the families of the residents, treated Lewis and I like hired help, as if we were there to cook and serve them. They forgot that we were volunteers and forgot the purpose behind our visits. We were certainly not there for them. We didn't allow ourselves to get affected too much by their ignorance, however, and we reminded each other often to always see the big picture. Lewis didn't like the way the staff spoke to the residents. I tried to make him feel better and told him that that was probably the way some of the residents needed to be spoken to. For a lot of them, anger, resentment and, often, rage, preceded resignation.

Most of the time, our simple presence was enough for the dying. We sat and listened to their stories and didn't care that some of the stories made no sense at all or that we had heard the same story many times before. Some asked to be read to and sang to. Some even asked me to write letters to loved ones on their behalf. Many asked to have their hands held, and for me to simply look into their eyes as we sat in silence. People who are dying crave human touch. I often massaged the resident's hands, exchanging energy and holding space in stillness.

Occasionally profound conversations emerged. The most interesting conversations were with the younger patients in their thirties and forties, and they all possessed a profound clarity at the end of their days.

They all admitted that a year prior, they would never have imagined that they would be on their deathbed. They were completely blind-sided by their illness. When I got to know the residents, a similar theme emerged. Nearly all of them had regrets. When I asked them what they would do differently, they expressed the common themes again and again. The following is my paraphrasing of these conversations and themes.

I wish I had the courage to disappoint my family so I could have lived the life that I wanted to live. I wish I wasn't so afraid of upsetting my father. I would have travelled the world after completing university. I would have chosen a different career. My father wanted me to become a lawyer and so I followed in his footsteps. I hated being a lawyer. I was stressed all the time. Depression was a familiar friend. I wanted to be a photographer and a travel writer. I wanted to be free. If I had my time over I would have done so many things differently.

I have so many dreams unfulfilled. My whole life, I was the 'Gonna Guy' – 'When this happens, I'm gonna do this. When this happens, I'm gonna do that. Only when this happens, then I'm gonna, gonna, gonna.' And I never did any of it. If I knew I would die so soon, I wouldn't have delayed my dreams. I wouldn't have put everyone else's happiness before my own. Now it's too late.

I wish I laughed more and wasn't so angry and judgemental all the time. My life was miserable. I was a misery. I wish I had more fun. I wish I had made the effort to do the work on myself and change my patterns and behaviours. If I had done that, I probably would have had more friends and been able to create more meaningful relationships. I wish I had the courage to let the toxic fake friends go sooner. I wasted too much time with the wrong people. Where are they now?

I wish I hadn't worked so hard. I loved my business, I loved working, but I let it take up too much of my time. I was working for the future. I wrongly assumed that I'd live into my eighties at least. I wish I lived a more exciting life – taken more vacations,

embraced more adventures ... enjoyed the little things. I wish
I spent more quality time with my wife, my children, my family
and my friends. I worked so hard all my life and for what? For
what? It kills my heart to know how difficult it will be for them
when I am gone.

I wished I married the woman I truly loved. I broke Bonnie's heart.
I married the woman my parents told me to marry and we were
never really happy. They tell me Bonnie never got over the pain
I caused her. I will ask for her forgiveness in my final hours.

I wish I wasn't so stubborn and hateful. I held onto grudges and
refused to forgive. I wish I had had the strength to let that shit go.
I wish I had the courage to tell the people around me that I loved
them. I wish I made happiness my priority instead of bitterness
and revenge. I know for sure that is what made me sick. Anger is
the selfish bastard that has robbed me of precious time.

Someone once told me the definition of hell: 'On my last day on
earth, the man I became will meet the man I could have been.'

'If only' were the words that I heard most often from the dying, and
these must be the two saddest words in the world. I watched as the
pain of regret accelerated the residents' decline. Regret for the things
they had done had alleviated over time, but it was the regret for the
things that they did *not* do that left them the most heartbroken. Too
often, they had loved, but they did not say so. It was the words left
unsaid, the deeds left undone and the person they did not become
that hurt them the most.

The Dalai Lama, when asked what surprised him most about humanity, answered,

Man. Because he sacrifices his health in order to make money.
Then he sacrifices money to recuperate his health. And then he
is so anxious about the future that he does not enjoy the present;
the result being that he does not live in the present or the future;
he lives as if he is never going to die, and then he dies having
never really lived.

When we can always see the big picture, we are charged and ready for whatever life throws our way. When we know where we are going, we know what we need to take with us. We are brave and confident to chart our own course to the destiny that we desire. When we always see the big picture, we can strive to achieve the worthy goals that tie to our passion and our life's purpose, and not get bogged down stressing needlessly about the petty things that don't matter. When we can always see the big picture, we can rise to the demands of any situation and enjoy the journey, with determination, playfulness and joy.

At the end of our lives, we will not be remembered by how many awards we won or how much money we have made. We will be remembered by how many people we assisted, the impact we made, the lives we changed, and how we helped to push humanity forward. The continued fulfilment of the pursuit of our infinite potential is what creates lasting happiness. It is the expansion of our consciousness and our continued mastery that creates for us a fulfilling life. Happiness and fulfilment in who we have become, the wealth we have acquired, the good deeds we have achieved for the world, the health and vitality that we wake up with every single day, and the love, admiration and respect from those around us.

SO HOW DO YOU CREATE THE BIG PICTURE FOR YOURSELF?

Redefining your happiness and seeing the big picture starts with you. Sit quietly somewhere you won't be disturbed. Be still. Inquire deeply and ask yourself these four intimate questions. The answers will help you to create big picture thinking and get clear on your personal priorities.

1. *How would I like to live this day if it were my last day on Earth?*
   Spend 60 seconds writing down the answers to this question, including what you would like to do, and who you would like to be.

2. *What would I like my friends to say about me at my funeral?* Write a paragraph on this.

3. *What would I like my work colleagues or employees to say about me at my funeral?* Write a paragraph on these things.

4. *What would I like my closest family members to say about me at my funeral?* Write a final paragraph on this.

You will find that the intention behind these snapshot answers are actually your own. They are your soul's calling. Now you can zero in on your priorities and become aware of what is truly important to you and those you hold dear.

'The Way' Secret #2

FULFILMENT IS THE
NEW CURRENCY

Yesterday I was clever, I wanted to change the world; today I am wise, I am changing myself.

—Rumi

The Way of the Spiritual Entrepreneur is a journey of continual change and evolution, just as the world is in constant change around us. We must always look for new ways to grow and evolve. This is what will give us the competitive edge in business and in life.

CONSISTENTLY CHANGE WHO YOU ARE

Every next level of your life will demand a new version of you. At every milestone, you must strive to always see the big picture and become a new person. Yes, you must literally change your character and change who you are. This is one of the missing components for many entrepreneurs. We are here on this earth to do one thing, and that is to evolve ... and to do it with joy. Science tells us that if we do not change who we are, we are not breaking the old neuro-circuitry that defines our old familiar self. If we are not deliberately changing who we are, we are not creating new genes and firing new neuropathways to increase our quality of character, our quality of life and its longevity. If we choose to remain the same person, we are stunting our growth, our joy and our evolution.

You cannot change who you are by simply your changing your hairstyle or your clothes. You can only change who you are by changing who you are. The person I am today is not the same person I was six months ago. The person I am in six months' time will be different to the person I am now. Every six months, I strive to deliberately change my character and shift gears to increase my energy and my drive. If you change your energy, you will change your life.

I continually strive to become more disciplined, more relentless and more skilled, while at the same time, I yearn for new chapters of strength, freedom and serenity. I hunger for new seasons of contribution and adventure, as well as surrender. I am continually reinventing myself. I am continually rewriting my story. I am continually redesigning my destiny. I am continually challenging the existing paradigms and transcending the status quo so that I can become the woman I am destined to be. Not the person 'they' told me I should be.

Personal development cannot happen unless personal disruption happens first. The work we do on ourselves proceeds layer by layer, from the most external forms of personality to the inner core of our being.

JUST AS WE EVOLVE, SO TOO MUST OUR BUSINESSES

In 2008, Red Lantern decided to grow up a little. Deeply affected by the multitude of awards and accolades we'd received, we realised that as restaurateurs, as business people, as parents and as human beings, we owed a social responsibility to our colleagues, our patrons and, especially, our environment. We realised that as leaders in our industry, we had the power to make a difference. Having children was a particularly massive wake up call for us. And so, we set ourselves a new goal and committed to a new mission: to leave as light an environmental footprint as possible, while staying true to our Vietnamese origins. We retrained the thinking of our team members and changed our philosophies and business model. We got rid of suppliers who couldn't tell us the provenance of our produce and we engaged with new, more integral suppliers. But our timing could not have been worse. We decided to do all of this smack-bang in the middle of the global financial crisis! While other restaurants were closing down, we had no choice but to raise our prices because of the extra cost of organic and sustainable produce.

Overnight we lost a whole lot of customers – those who still believed that Vietnamese food should be cheap. 'Cheap and cheerful,' they call it. The empty seats left us deflated and dispirited. Our cash flow became strained and, for the first time in Red Lantern history, we wondered if we would make enough money to pay our staff, our bills, our taxes, our rent and our many suppliers. Few people realise the immense number of outgoings it takes to run a full-service restaurant. On some occasions, I had no choice but to pay staff wages as well as rent from my own personal savings. We were in pain. But our purpose was too strong to go back on our vision. If our upbringing had taught us one thing time and time again, it was to never, ever give up – and that, if we dig deep enough and remain optimistic, the solution will always arrive for us.

Optimism versus positive thinking

In the face of adversity, choose optimism over positive thinking every time.

Why? Because an optimistic brain is far more capable of shifting us forward than a brain that is stuck in fear, blame and excuses. Positive thinking is a bandaid solution for the uncomfortable reality of a current situation. The positive thinker tries to shine a positive light on a negative situation, but it is scientifically proven that positive thinking doesn't work. It is unnatural for human beings to be positive and happy twenty-four hours a day, seven days a week.

Positive thinking doesn't actually help you as much as you might think. Trying to maintain only positive visions of the future while pursuing your goals will hinder your progress in achieving them. It is unwise to try to be positive all the time and, in a business setting, this can be counterproductive. We have moments of inner peace and we have moments of inner turmoil. If we have inner peace twenty-four seven, we will stagnate. Inner turmoil makes us innovate, create and recalibrate. Inner turmoil inspires us to buckle down and make the strong, persistent effort that is necessary to find the solution and realise a feasible goal. The overemphasis on happiness at the expense of sadness might paradoxically limit your choices rather than increase them. Melancholy is an essential part of a full life.

Emotions aren't bad – we learn from experiencing the full gamut of emotions. The so-called negative experiences and instincts are not to be denied; they are simply a part of life. The question is this: for how long will you hold onto that emotion? If you hold onto the emotions long enough, they become your identity.

The Spiritual Entrepreneur possesses emotional mastery and allows themselves to sit inside the darkness for only a short period of time in order to learn from it. They understand that without the darkness, the light would not exist. As Carl Jung said, 'One does not become enlightened by imagining figures of light but by making the darkness conscious.' A natural balance exists in all things: life and death, good and bad, happiness and sadness, pleasure and pain. The very idea that you should focus on positives and ignore negatives is not only delusional but also a recipe for disaster.

The Spiritual Entrepreneur has mastered the skills to come out of the darkness and get back into alignment to do what needs to be done. This is what optimism is about. Grit, calm courage and resilience, sprinkled with a large dose of 'nevergiveupology', can also turn any situation around. The optimist always sees the big picture and holds strong the belief and faith in a better future. It is the absolute knowing that all will be amazing – even if things are not currently so amazing. Scottish philosopher Thomas Carlyle backed this up when he wrote,

Permanence, perseverance and persistence in spite of all obstacles, discouragements, and impossibilities: it is this that in all things distinguish themselves the strong soul from the weak.

Persistence is a key characteristic of successful entrepreneurs, as is the ability to pivot for a higher calling when it is aligned with what we truly want. It is easy to be optimistic when everything is going great. It is crucial to be optimistic when things are not going great. In order to remain optimistic when times are tough, we must be at our most diligent at being aware of the story that we are consciously telling ourselves. It is important to escape the perspective of blame, shame, overwhelm and despair. Martin Seligman writes that flexible learned optimism combined with true grit will help us to rise above pessimism and the depression that accompanies negative thoughts. Optimism is a way of thinking that embraces the reality of the current situation and then imagines a situation from a higher level of mind in search of a better perspective. Optimism requires your brain to come up with the actions needed to shift to a better situation.

The optimist knows in their gut that their beliefs and the words they use to speak to themselves and others have a lot to do with what shows up in their life. The optimist knows that it is their thoughts and their feelings that create their destiny. What you focus on the most will always manifest in your life. It is the law.

Through habit, the victim will focus on the cost. The A-player will focus on the value. The pessimist will focus first on all the ways it won't work. The 'possibilitarian' will think of all the ways to make it work. The optimist will combine high-level thinking with elevated emotions such as hope, joy, gratitude, love, playfulness and compassion to get them to where they want to go faster. Elevated emotions are the secret ingredient. Elevated emotions combined with high-level thinking will raise our vibration to meet new levels of infinite possibility. It is during the most difficult times that it is of the utmost importance to keep strong the gatekeepers of our mind and our heart. If we choose optimism and focus all of our energy on the things that will get us to where we want to be, we will succeed faster. The brain science behind optimism proves it far more powerful than positive thinking.

HOW DETERMINED YOU ARE, DETERMINES YOUR OUTCOME

During the difficult time we faced in 2008, it was of the utmost importance for us to stay away from the majority of our industry peers – the ones who complained all the time and blamed everyone and everything else instead of taking action toward a better future. The constant complaining about how tough the economy was and how 'tight' the customers had become bored us, and did not serve us in any way. This wasn't the quality of peers we wanted to surround ourselves with during this tumultuous time. These people were afraid to fail and their fear caused them to do nothing. In business as in life – if you do nothing, you are 100 per cent guaranteed to fail. Fear like this means you end up with the very thing you fear. Alternatively, any action you take toward the big picture that you hold in your mind and your heart will immediately increase your chance of success. Fate loves the fearless.

While everyone was going in one direction, we at Red Lantern chose the opposite direction. While everyone else was downgrading their dreams to match their reality, we upgraded our belief to match our vision. Steve Jobs put it this way: 'You can't look at the competition and say you're going to do better. You have to look at the competition and say you're going to do it differently.' Every day we reminded ourselves of the big picture. Even though we were doing it tough, we didn't give up on what we believed in. Mark implemented initiatives ranging from waterless wok systems to low-energy lighting and energy offsets – which ultimately resulted in considerable cost savings in the long run. We ensured most of the vegetables served at Red Lantern come from the Sydney basin, within 45 to 60 minutes from the restaurant. When it came to protein, Mark focused on quality over quantity. He wanted the produce to shine.

There is a perception of Vietnamese food that it is cheap, and it can be if you disregard many things including the quality of service as well as the quality and provenance of the produce. We wanted to elevate Vietnamese cuisine, not devalue it. Mark started to talk to different suppliers so he could form relationships and use free-range and organic produce where he could. It was a deliberate journey where we were trying to provide a point of difference for ourselves and our customers.

Elon Musk once said that the one thing that defines a true entrepreneur is their high pain tolerance. While the average entrepreneur wants to avoid as much pain as possible, we know that in business, and especially if you have multiple businesses, pain is inevitable but suffering is a choice. The people who master everything in this world are the people who take responsibility when they fail. And when they fail, they reflect and they learn. When they learn the truth, they remember the lesson and they evolve. Your best teacher is your last mistake. The Spiritual Entrepreneur knows that they alone have the responsibility and the power to turn the situation around. A business that can dominate during tough times is a business that can crush it.

You cannot win the war outside if you are losing your inner war.

Intensity of action and intensity of mind breeds intense rewards.

As we continued to do the inner work and to consciously live in an elevated state of being, something miraculous happened. Within a few months, our outer world started to respond to our inner world. Our reality became a reflection of our mind. We started to see new faces at Red Lantern. Better faces. More joyful faces. More grateful faces. More appreciative customers started to hear about our commitment to food provenance and sustainability. Red Lantern's fresh, free-range fare, which focused on promoting local producers, started to attract a new clientele. Those who, because of the state of the economy, had to take a step or two down from their usual spend bracket. Red Lantern wasn't cheap but we weren't expensive either. We sat beautifully in the middle and offered delicious modern Vietnamese cuisine with a social conscience. This made our new and remaining clientele very happy. Our restaurant filled up again with higher quality customers. The Universe responded with something even better than what we had prayed for.

We had taken a massive gamble. We believed in something higher than ourselves. We wanted to leave a legacy for our kids and an important message for the next generation. We took a big risk during a risky time and it paid off. Thank god it paid off!

Those who find meaning and purpose even in the most horrendous circumstances are far more resilient to 'suffering' than those who do not. We refused to be victims of our circumstances or of our past. We were free to view things differently and added the meaning that most empowered us.

And have we experienced other challenges and difficulties along the way? Of course we have. Over the years, we have survived a multitude of economic downturns, some so severe we have fallen to our knees. And did each struggle require the same level of mind and the same consistency and intensity of inner work to rise above it and come out the victor?

Yes.

Professionally and socially, we have experienced much racism thrown at us. Personally, I have experienced a great deal of sexism as well – in the form of blatant discrimination as well as unconscious bias. Not only am I a woman, but I am also an Asian woman. Not only am I an Asian woman, but I am also a short Asian woman. Jokes aside and truth be known, I do not let these things bother me. While I am aware of such issues, I do not subscribe to them. Why would I want to waste my valuable time and my valuable energy being bothered by the ignorant opinion of others and the external forces I cannot control? I would rather spend my valuable time and my valuable energy counting my blessings. Nothing will boost your overall levels of happiness long term than 'counting your blessings' for both supportive and challenging events. I would rather spend my valuable time and my valuable energy being in a state of gratitude and appreciation, and focusing on the things I can control. It is my internal ecology that matters most – and also, I don't do 'victim' well.

According to Robert Kiyosaki, 'The size of your success is measured by the strength of your desire, the size of your dream and how you handle disappointment along the way.'

There is too much giving up in this world. The Spiritual Entrepreneur remains persistent to attain calm courage, resilience and grit. The Spiritual Entrepreneur remains optimistic and becomes a master at their craft – the master of their life.

GETTING CLEAR ON YOUR PRIORITIES AND CREATING THE PRINCIPLES THAT DEFINE YOU

From big picture thinking, we create life priorities.

From life priorities, we create our life principles.

From life principles, we create daily actions.

From daily actions, we create daily habits.

From daily habits, we create our Quadrant 4 destiny.

Answering the big picture questions from the last chapter will help you to consciously discover your true priorities. At the end of the day, are you going to care about whether or not you lived in that five-bedroom house with the swimming pool? Chances are, at the end of the day you'll care more about upscaling your character, becoming a better person, being healthy, being more loving, helping the people around you and pushing humanity forward in some way.

Your true priorities are the ones that you will eventually arrive at, of your own accord – consciously through your own soul searching and questioning on your life journey. Before that, your priorities were acquired unconsciously, handed down to you by your parents, relatives, teachers and carers. You adopted these values as children, when you were simply too young to apply a filter of reason.

In this section, I give you some examples of life priorities and then show you how to convert them to one-word principles. These principles will become your life's non-negotiable foundational building blocks.

Some examples of life priorities are:

- To keep fit, healthy and feeling vital
- To spend quality time with the people I love
- To make time to contemplate and reflect
- To surround myself with great people
- To deepen my spiritual connection
- To uplift those who I come in contact with and leave them with a sense of increase
- To live my full potential

As per this example, aim for seven life priorities. Let's now take the preceding list of life priorities and convert them into one-word principles:

- To keep fit, healthy and feeling vital becomes HEALTH
- To spend quality time with the people I love becomes LOVE
- To make time to contemplate and reflect becomes INNER PEACE

- To surround myself with great people becomes INFLUENCE
- To deepen my spiritual connection becomes SPIRITUAL
- To uplift those who I come in contact with and leave them with a sense of increase becomes INSPIRATION
- To live my full potential becomes EVOLVE

At the end of this exercise we are left with seven words. These seven words are our principles, the foundation of our life. They are our self-determined, consciously chosen laws, by which we live our life each day.

From my priorities, I can extrapolate my life principles.

We convert our priorities into principles for two reasons. Having only a few words makes our principles simple and easy to remember. In times of stress, these principles then become a touchstone that helps to keep our life on point.

Once we have crystallised our true priorities and distilled them into principles, we now convert them into actions that we perform daily. Why daily? Because we have already determined that nothing is more important than *living the life you want now!* The actions you take each day create the results of your life. We simply have no reason to postpone. Nothing takes precedence over our principles.

Until you understand specifically what you truly value most, what truly inspires you, who you truly are, and what your true purpose is, a completely inspired and fulfilled life will elude you. If you don't fill your days intentionally with the things that are inspiring to you, they can fill up with the things that aren't. So why not fill your days with the things that are of highest value to you? Otherwise, you end up filling your days living out someone else's values and priorities and not your own. This is a recipe for resentment, frustration and quiet desperation. Your life is right now. It's not later. You might as well decide to start enjoying your life right now, because it's not ever going to get better than right now – until it gets better than right now. Live your truth so that thankfulness and gratitude fills your heart, energises your body and clarifies your mind each and every day.

Converting a principle to a daily action

Let's use the examples of principles that we've been working with. Asking yourself what actions might promote each principle could give you the following:

What are two things I can do today to promote HEALTH?

1. Go for a run along the beach.
2. Drink a mixed berry and spirulina smoothie.

What are two things I can do today to promote LOVE?

1. Share a meal with a dear friend or family member.
2. Spend time connecting with my children.

What are two things I can do today to experience INNER PEACE?

1. Take the dog for a walk through the park.
2. Sit under my favourite tree and pray.

What are two things I can do today to increase my INFLUENCE?

1. Call a mentor or a mentee to see what new things they're up to.
2. Write a blog or share a thought-provoking point of view on social media.

What are two things I can do today to nurture my SPIRITUALITY?

1. Meditate for 30 minutes.
2. Journal ten things for which I am grateful.

What are two things I can do today to INSPIRE?

1. Give three compliments to my employees.
2. Spend an hour writing my book.

What are two things I can do today that will contribute to my EVOLUTION?

1. Read for 60 minutes on a topic that will fuel my brain.
2. Teach someone the things that I have learned.

Self-discipline is the centre of all material success. How you do anything is how you do everything. Your rituals define you. Without self-mastery, we are slaves to fear.

Choose the actions that are in your best interest. This includes the thoughts you think. The words you speak. The foods you eat. The people you associate with. Be impeccable with your word. Eat like you love yourself, move like you love yourself, speak like you love yourself, and act like you love yourself. Dream big and your behaviour will follow. Think small and you'll play small. People fail because they make bad decisions. They think that there is too much transformation to be had in too little time. They neglect to see the big picture and drift into overwhelm. Making mistakes is a part of the process. Success does not teach us anything, failure does. Understand that your life is a marathon, it is not a sprint. It is not about the size of your title but the depth of your commitment. Listen to your intuition and follow your heart. Don't be afraid to fail. Failure is only a word. Many would argue that there is no such thing as failure – only feedback. As long as you grow, you will be happy. Progress is the one thing makes us humans truly happy.

Failure should be our teacher, not our undertaker.
Failure is delay, not defeat.
It is a temporary detour, not a dead end.
—Denis Waitley

Live your truth and become fearless

Success is a creative pursuit. Success is a reflection of healthy esteem. Abundance, peace, love, joy, health, happiness – the best elements of your life do not just show up out of nowhere. You need to create and cultivate them. Create your life the way you envision it and don't allow anyone to distort your perception. If what you choose to do does not bring you joy, it is not your truth. Pivot, and try again. The quality of your performance depends on the strength of your practice. When you commit daily to performing actions that nurture your consciously created life principles, get ready for a quantum leap in your baseline level of happiness. Why? Because the actions you are taking are in complete accord with your big picture life values. It is impossible to go wrong because you are completely aligned, completely congruent. Internal congruence leads to lasting happiness because everything in your life feels meaningful and rich. Every thought and every action is consciously aligned with your life's deepest priorities. When you take the high-priority actions that are truly most meaningful to you, your self-worth, self-esteem and self-confidence increase, making you fearless – as though you can overcome any impediment that seeks to block your chosen path.

Over the weeks of performing your principle-centred actions, you will find that your actions will become instinctual and habitual. And, before you know it, you have successfully converted your daily actions into daily habits, and you are doing it with joy because you are in alignment with your true values. Your habits are pristine reflections of your values. When this happens, you are progressing along your personal happiness continuum. You are slowly but surely increasing your subjective happiness score. When you consistently set your goals to match your highest values, you will increase the chances of achieving them. When you live with your highest values on a daily basis, you raise your certainty of success. When you raise your certainty of success, you will continue to pursue the challenges that inspire you and, inevitably, you will invite more love, more joy and more fulfilment into your heart. You will require no outside motivation, no incentives – nothing on the outside extrinsically to fulfil it. It will become an intrinsic value.

When the quality of your emotions is elevated to match the destiny that you desire ahead of time, you will experience happiness and fulfilment on a daily basis and it will only be a matter of time before your outer world responds to your inner world. It is only a matter of time before sustainable financial abundance starts to flow into your orbit. And indeed it is sustainable and indeed your happiness is lasting because you are living your life in harmony with your soul every single day. What you dwell on will determine your destiny. It is the law.

OUR PURPOSE IS TO EVOLVE

Many of us think that we will be happy when we finally reach the destination and win the prize – so much so that we forget to enjoy the journey. The journey is in fact the destination because the journey is what you spend all your time doing. The journey is the beautiful string of magic moments all tied together, and if you can be content in the continuous moments that you have purposely designed, your contentment and happiness ceases to be anchored in winning the prize. The getting of the prize comes and goes in the blink of an eye. It is the journey that will be remembered.

We all go on the journey, and the entrepreneur's journey is assured to be a tumultuous one. The beautiful part is that we all have free will and we all get to choose. You get to choose if you want to travel on the glorious journey with joy or with misery. Your choice. If you get clear on your priorities and create the principles that define you, you will find yourself enjoying the journey as well as the destination. This is when you reach Quadrant 4 happiness and financial abundance becomes your destiny.

Jay Abraham writes:

> *Most people think that when they acquire wealth, success, getting the biggest house, starting the fastest growing company, marrying the prettiest wife, making the Forbes List, whatever, they think that's going to transform them. They think the heavens are going to open, the angels are going to sing, euphoria's going to happen, and all their worries will just disappear. But that's not how it goes. It's anticlimactic. All of that, it doesn't change anything. I finally found one answer that's redefined my life. And here it is … the meaning of life is the process. The meaning of life is in conversations with a waiter or a janitor or an executive at the top company. It's all in the process and, in my case, it's in my commitment to add value anytime I interact with anybody. If you can get that in alignment, find a way to help someone else while you help yourself, then everything else flows.*

What we desire is deliberately placed out of reach so that we can become the person it takes to obtain it. Awakening is not changing who you are, but discarding who you are not and then designing who you want to become. You become the author of your life when you get clear on your values and commit daily to performing the actions that nurture your consciously created life principles. The alignment of your work with your core values is the key to fulfilment. Fulfilment is the new currency. Fulfilment is the key to lasting happiness.

You become the master of your life when you learn to control where your attention goes, and when you place great value on your time, your energy and your attention. Be disciplined to what you respond and react to. Not everyone deserves your time, your energy and your attention. When you deliberately choose high-level thinking and match it with elevated emotions, you will raise your vibration and all that is not in alignment will leave your life. When you have decided on your priorities and principles, when your focus is unrelenting and you can shut out the noise, don't be surprised how quickly the Universe will move with you. Life responds to the quality of your thoughts and the quality of your character. Never underestimate the power of a decision. As you rise, everything in your orbit will ascend with you. Life gets very exciting when you learn that you have the power to speak things into existence.

‘The Way’ Secret #3

BE A CONTAGION

Our destiny changes with our thought; we shall become what we wish to become, do what we wish to do, when our habitual thought corresponds with our desire. Don't wait for extraordinary opportunities. Seize common occasions and make them great. Weak men wait for opportunities; strong men make them.

—Orison Swett Marden

I KNOW WHAT FEAR SMELLS LIKE

My father had three instruments of torture. The first was a stiff and shiny billiard stick, the second was a flexible cane whip, and the third (and most effective) was fear. If someone were to ask me now what I remember most about my childhood, it would be the overwhelming stench of fear. I know what fear smells like. Fear dominated every day of my childhood. Fear followed me everywhere that I went. Fear stayed with me every day. I cannot remember a time when fear did not lurk over my shoulder. Fear seeped through every window, rose up from each shiny floorboard and spilled through the dead cracks in our walls. It hovered over our beds while we were sleeping.

Twice a year from the ages of seven to thirteen, my brothers and I brought home our school reports. For every B grade, my father caned us once. For every C grade, he caned us twice. This ritual required us to lay flat on our stomachs and not budge a millimetre until he was done. Blow after blow hacking at the flesh of our buttocks and thighs. We swallowed the pain without dropping a tear, with teeth clenched and fists squeezed tight until our knuckles turned white. I sometimes stared out the window and wondered what the neighbours would think if they ever heard us scream. What did it matter? To shed a tear or release a whimper at any time throughout this ritual meant a further beating to nullify our weakness. I cried only in private, knowing that the pain and bruising usually got worse before it got any better.

When my father's wrath relented a little, and as we lay before him in a bloody heap, he threw us a dollar for every A. Every day for the seven days leading up to report day, my father would lay out his instruments of torture in full view for us kids to see. Every day, we embraced and comforted each other. We stood strong and whispered quietly into the other's ear, the single-minded words of courage and optimism that only kids who experienced the world like we did would understand. 'Be brave. It will be over soon. Be brave.' The reality of our lives was unfair, unkind and affectionless. Over the years, our skin grew thick and our pain tolerance high. My father had successfully created four tough working machines. No parent could have wished for better children. We were disciplined, obedient, hardworking, sensitive, caring, polite and always respectful. Mentally and physically we were strong. Emotionally and spiritually we were a mess.

My father was angry all the time. He had an anger in him that neither he nor anyone else could explain. He was like a faulty pressure cooker, always on the boil – a rolling heat building up inside, waiting to explode in the most destructive way. One of my father's well used and memorable quotes was 'I created you, and I have the power to destroy you'.

What problems my father must have had within himself to treat his innocent children with such contempt – his explosive anger completely out of proportion to any incident at hand. Perhaps the hurdles of adaptation to a new country so soon after the war proved too difficult to cope with. Perhaps the accumulated weight of responsibility from running multiple businesses grew too much for him to bear. Maybe the acute sciatica pain strained his patience and drained him of all his energy. On several occasions, I witnessed my father offload his anger on my mother. The first time I saw him inflict permanent physical damage was when I was six years old. In a rage, he smashed a chair across her face and broke her nose.

'I had nightmares,' my father tells me now. 'The same dream, over and over. I am back in Vietnam planning for our escape. The dream is so real. I am back in the water day after day with nowhere to go, and then I wake up.' My father had constant flashbacks to the war. Part of his job as a lieutenant in artillery was to go back to the scene of a battle and count the dead bodies. It was his duty to assess the damage so as to better calculate his aim for next time. 'I don't know how many I killed; one shell killed so many.' The scars from his own bullet wounds resemble a question mark down the length of his spine.

Many of my father's friends, with whom he fought alongside in the war, came to him with the same sorts of flashbacks – some memories far more horrific. Visitors came to ask for his advice about the laws and the language in their new country. Some hung around our restaurant all day to ease feelings of loneliness and isolation. They too struggled to cope with the scars of past experiences, finding it hard to function, let alone provide for their families. Like my father, many showed signs of depression and PTSD. I once asked my father if he would agree that he and his friends might have benefitted from seeking professional guidance – if not to allow some sort of healing, then at least to acknowledge the darkness that festered within. In typical fashion, my father responded, 'What for? What was the point? We just got on with it.'

MY ONLY COMPETITION IS MY POTENTIAL

One morning, after the rain and just before December, I packed a single suitcase, said goodbye to my brothers and walked out the tired front door. I was seventeen and I had officially become a 'runaway'. With the courage of soldiers, my brothers then ventured out to the restaurant to face the firing line. They presented my father with the farewell letter that I had hand written – a soft and compassionate letter outlining all the reasons I had to leave the family home. My brothers told my father that they had 'found' the letter after 'discovering' that I had gone.

At the restaurant, my father hastily read my words and put them in his pocket. He ordered my brothers to join him at the table. He picked up four square stainless steel napkin dispensers and placed them neatly on top of one another. With steel in his voice, he told them, 'These represent each one of you.' He pointed to each dispenser as he spoke, resting his finger on the bottom dispenser. 'This one is your sister, she is meant to be the foundation for the four of you.' After a long and deliberate pause, he took a sudden violent swing at the bottom dispenser, sending it flying through the air, smashing it against the tiled wall. As the top three dispensers came crashing to the ground, he shouted, 'Instead, she has chosen to wreck the family home!' My brothers tell me that the restaurant was full of customers that day, and that he had digested not one word of my letter. 'She is wrong,' he said, 'to do what she has done.'

With the help of a close friend and the support of my brothers, I went into hiding. My father ordered his men to search for me. My brothers, who always knew of my whereabouts, warned me by phone if my father or any of his henchmen came close to finding me. He had spread the word that there could only be two reasons for my leaving: one, that I had become a drug addict too ashamed to face the world; or, two, that I had fallen pregnant to the phantom boyfriend that he had conjured in his head.

For me, life was also about survival. In order to survive, I could not allow myself, not even for moment, to think about the tremendous shame that I had dumped upon my family. The months passed slowly as I moved around to avoid detection. Truly fearing for my life, I hid in the quiet beach town of Newcastle, north of Sydney – one of the last places anyone would think of looking. But my spirit grew weary of living in fear and my body tired of being on the run. I made up my mind to return to Sydney and get myself a university degree. By this time, I had found new strength. My fear of the future was nothing compared to my fear of the past. Even so, out of habit, I would look over my shoulder everywhere that I went, paranoid that familiar faces were following me.

I put myself through university and completed a BA Communications, and attended AFTRS (the Australian Film, Television and Radio School). Looking back, I find it amusing that, even years after leaving home, I still felt compelled to inform my father of my academic achievements. Every semester I sent home to my father my university reports. I would cut away my home address so that he wouldn't know where I lived, but I wanted him to know about my achievements, and know that there were some things I would never forget.

But there comes a time when you need to overcome your fears by looking at them in the face. And for the sake of my mother, and for the sake of my brothers, and for all the shame I had dumped on my family in the years that I was away, I reluctantly reconciled with my father. Out of duty I would go home to visit, and I hated those visits. I hated the sense of claustrophobia and suffocation I always felt in his presence. The meetings were always stifled and false. But what I hated the most about those visits was the overwhelming realisation that I had grown up to be just like him. I too was angry all the time. Angry at my friends, angry at my work colleagues, angry at the world, angry at myself. Angry people are highly skilled at noticing all that is wrong. For many years, anger was the default emotion I ran to – anger and judgement. I was constantly in 'error detection mode'. This was how I was brought up. This was all I knew. This is what my parents had downloaded onto me.

My neuroscience teacher refers to this as the 'Right Wrong Virus' – a mind operating system that has error-detection and judgement at its core. This is essentially a prevalent human condition. Those who judge the most are secretly the ones who feel the most judged.

Do you know why Buddha sits on a Lotus Flower?

I carried this anger with me for many years but when my husband and I decided to have a child, I was determined that this cycle end with me. I was determined to not pass on my anger to the next generation.

So, in 2007 I landed a book deal … to write a recipe book and memoir about my family. As I'm writing this book, my fears returned. As I'm writing this book, I'm thinking, *How am I possibly going to survive my father's reaction to this story?* The book is called *Secrets of the Red Lantern* and it's not meant to be a scathing account about my father. Instead, it's a beautiful story about personal freedom, family and hope. Ten chapters are included all up, and it was my intention to complete the book and give it to my father in its entirety so that he could see the full arc of the story, and see what a beautiful story it really is. But in order to talk about the good stuff, we have to share some of the bad stuff that happened as well, right?

By the end of the fifth chapter, my father demands to read my story and I freak out. I freak out because he can't possibly read it now. It's not finished! The fifth chapter is also the worst chapter about my father. It is the most scathing account about him and he can't possibly read it now. It's not finished! But you don't say no to my father, and I had no choice but to hand over my unfinished manuscript. The story about his life written by his prodigal daughter. I didn't hear from my father for three months and I needed to hear from him. I needed to finish my book. I need to move on.

Fathers' Day came and I decided to go home and face the music. As I am driving home to Bonnyrigg (where my parents still lived), with my brand-new baby daughter, Mia, the nerves and anxiety overwhelm me as usual. Fear chokes me and I can hardly breathe. I'm not scared that he will hit me or do anything like that. We were past that stage in our lives. I'm scared because I'm about to do something that has never been done before. I'm about to confront my father to end this family's pattern. I'm about to face my fears to make things better than before.

So, I'm at the front door, and I've brought with me a case of my father's favourite red wine as a peace offering. My parents open the door and see Mia for the first time. They immediately take her from me. They kiss her, they cuddle her; they're so happy to see her and I can tell that they are in awe of her smallness. As I enter the house, I see that they have created a feast for me. The old family table is covered in traditional goodness – caramelised pork, tomato prawns, roast duck, and bitter melon soup. When we sit down to eat, I take a moment to find my centre. I sneak a peek at their faces and see a look in their eyes that I have never seen before. They're treating one another with a new softness and speaking to me with deliberate respect. 'I was wrong,' my father admits to me unexpectedly. The sound of those three foreign words – 'I was wrong' – make me sit up and pay attention.

'Do you know why Buddha sits on a lotus flower?' my father asks me.

I answer with caution, 'No, Dad. Why does Buddha sit on a lotus flower?'

In a voice so sad and serious, he responds, 'Nothing is as beautiful as a lotus flower. Out of watery chaos it grows, emerging from the depths of a muddy swamp and yet it remains pure and unpolluted. So pure you can eat it – all of it, the flowers, the seeds, the leaves, the roots, the petals. But the lotus flower has another characteristic. Its stalk you can easily bend but you cannot easily break. It has strong tenacious fibres that hold the plant together.' He takes a deep breath before continuing. 'My children are lotus flowers.' My silence enables him to carry on. 'Like the lotus flower, all of you have grown out of the mud of your origins. You have grown out of the aftermath of war. You have grown out of Cabramatta during its murkiest time – and you grew out of me. I am dirt. I am mud. I am shit. I am very lucky to have you all.'

Has it been a dream? Has my father really given me the moment I had waited over twenty years for? He has caught me by surprise — he has given me that and so much more. He hasn't given me an apology, but I didn't need an apology. The best apology is his changed behaviour. What my father gives me is acknowledgement — acknowledgment of the harm that he had inflicted. He tells me that, had he read the book ten years ago, he would have exploded. He is solemn when he concludes, 'But there is a right time and a right place for everything.'

THE UNIVERSE WILL ONLY HAND TO YOU WHAT IT KNOWS YOU CAN HANDLE

Secrets of the Red Lantern became an international bestseller and, in 2008, I was voted Debut Writer of The Year by the Australian book publishing industry. No-one was more surprised than I was. The book is hardly a literary masterpiece, but I wrote it from the heart. It is raw, it is dark and it is beautiful. I wrote it for my daughter, Mia, so that when she is old enough to want to read it, she can understand where I came from and what it took to get here. How was I to know that my story would change the lives of so many all around the world?

At home I have two large cardboard boxes overflowing with letters and copies of emails from people all over the world. Vietnam veterans wrote to share with me their own stories not dissimilar to that of my father's. They told me that they thought him a hero. I have received letters from survivors of domestic abuse, as well as from people who admitted that they were once racists but were no longer so after reading the book — because they now understood the circumstances of those they had judged. What surprised me the most was the plethora of letters I received from children of survivors of the holocaust. Same story, different war.

For a year, the publishers threw me head first in the very deep end of the writers' festival circuit, promoting the book at home and abroad.

'You must be your own marketing machine,' they told me. As a novice speaker and as a novice human being, I was untrained, unskilled and unevolved. Recounting my personal story on stage became excruciating – not only for myself, but also for the audience. Time and time again, the unhealed scars of the past snuck up from the recesses of my gut and lodged in my throat, leaving me speechless, trembling and traumatised on stage.

From a psychological perspective, trauma is defined as an experience that the mental psyche cannot integrate because it exceeds the capacity of the one who experiences it to absorb it. It is as if the traumatic event short-circuits the psyche. The psyche freezes on the trauma, mesmerised by the violence, unable to process it and caught in an abysmal suffering.

A good friend who came to see me speak told me in private that he felt like running on stage to slap me hard across the face just so that he could break the debilitating state that choked me and held me captive in front of the audience of hundreds. I had not dealt with the trauma. I did not have control over my emotions. The audience did not deserve to see me this way.

I made a decision that day that changed the course of my life. I knew that if I did not empower my life, something else or someone else will overpower it. With single-minded determination, I made a vow to myself to go in search of the best speaking coaches in the world, to help me master the craft. I never wanted to lose control on stage like that ever again. Two years later, having spoken in front of tens of thousands of people, and having practised for tens of thousands of hours as a keynote speaker, honing my skills and mastering my craft, my agents told me I had become one of the top female keynote speakers in Australia. In recent times, I have won the Australian Telstra Business Award for Medium Business and have been listed in Rare Birds: Australia's 50 Influential Women Entrepreneurs, and am included in Blackwell and Hobday's global recognition of *200 Women Who Will Change the Way You See the World*.

I do not write about my achievements to brag. It is not in my DNA to brag. I am not driven by praise, nor am I motivated by pride. Pride consumes the weak and kills their heart from within. I share my accomplishments to encourage you to realise the infinite possibilities when you do the inner work, as well as the outer work, with consistency. Good things do not come to those who wait. Good things come to those who put in the work every day. Good things come to those who hustle with persistency, and continually master the weapons of influence. Good things come to those who practice 'nevergiveupology' on a daily basis.

Looking back, I do not feel like a victim. I don't do victim. Looking back, I've realised if it had not been for all of the challenges that I have experienced, I would not be the person I am today. How was I to know that my greatest life obstacles would give me my greatest life opportunities? No, I have never seen myself as a victim. I believe that I am the lucky beneficiary of all the things that have happened for me. Can you imagine living in a world not of victims but of beneficiaries? These experiences have taught me independence and have made me strong.

Understanding that life is full of supportive as well as challenging circumstances (as well as people) can help us to appreciate the balancing power of the mind and can add to this state of equilibrium called fulfilment. Over the years I have learned that whoever has the most certainty around this concept rules the game. If there is meaning in life at all, then there must be meaning in suffering. Suffering ceases to be suffering at the moment it finds meaning. This is the point when we become unshakable. Being unshakable means possessing confidence, calm and courage in the face of any adversity. Confidence, calm and courage are contagious.

Through these life lessons, I have also learnt resilience and grit. I know my potential. I have discovered that I can take the most confronting parts of the human experience and turn them into opportunities to help others. Speaking, writing, teaching and enlightening is what I was put on this earth to do. To make a massive impact to a lot of people in a short period of time. I have, at last, found my purpose – my reason for being. I have spent years reflecting on what it all meant. I am now clear on the lessons. I know why I am here.

The meaning of life is to find your gift.
The purpose of life is to give it away.
—Pablo Picasso

Two common questions I get asked in my work as a coach and a mentor are, 'What is purpose? And how do I go about finding out what my purpose is?' The first thing I point out is that purpose is not a race. Discovering yourself, redefining yourself, evolving into who you are meant to be and discovering the reason why you are here takes time. I then expand my clients' definition of purpose. Our purpose is not our career or the job that we choose. Our purpose here on earth is to evolve, to come out of hiding and to stop pretending to be someone we are not. Our purpose is to become the true expression of the greatest vision that we hold for ourselves – our most authentic self, fully and completely, 100 per cent. Our purpose is to evolve and grow into our truth and to contribute these gifts to the world. We are what we share.

And how do we find our purpose? How do we tap into our true gifts and power? Look at what your life already demonstrates. A hidden order is at play here. Ask yourself, what is your reason for being? What are the values that you uphold that are true to you? Your highest values are your life's calling. Your values represent what is most important and meaningful to you. Your values underpin your everyday thoughts, decisions, behaviours and actions. Your values determine the results you get in life – both positive and negative. Your highest value is your purpose. Your burning desire is your purpose. It is the desire that burns so deep that you do not fear the sacrifices that you will need to make to get to where you want to be. When you can embrace the pain as well as the pleasure to reach your goal and purpose, then you will know it is your highest value … and you won't mind one bit needing to divorce yourself from the crowd in order to achieve it.

Reverend Michael Beckwith puts it this way:

Behind every obstacle there is a question trying to be asked,
and behind every question there is an answer trying to reveal
itself. And behind every answer there is an action trying to express

itself, and behind every action there is a way of life trying to be born. If you ask the powerful questions, you will get the powerful answers, and the whispers of wisdom from the universe will reveal itself to you. You will start to recall in the past the things you were good at. You will recall experiences when you felt elated and in flow. And then you will lean into those things so deep that you fall in love with it. If you fall in love with something deep enough, it will reveal its secrets to you.

And how will you know when you have found the answer? You will know because you will ignite. You will sparkle. You will feel alive like you have never felt before. You will feel charged with a new energy, a new hunger, a new life vision. You will wake up every day in spirit – inspired with a fire in your belly and a bounce in your step, over-flowing with creative energy. And then you will surrender to it. And once you surrender to it, abundant opportunities, and connections and happiness and wealth will come your way because you are in alignment with your true calling. And the opportunities that will enter your life will be so mystical and magical and profound that you will have no doubt a hidden order is at play, and that you have been touched by the Divine.

And you are not limited to only one purpose in life that you have to 'discover'. You have the freedom to choose. You get to choose. So stop searching and start choosing!

The Spiritual Entrepreneur is ambitious, resilient, open-minded and audience driven. Their work has a lasting impact because of its relevance to their audience. And, of course, their pursuits must make money. The Spiritual Entrepreneur has transcended the spiritual bypass that money is evil. Money is energy made up of consciousness just like everything else. The Spiritual Entrepreneur enjoys financial abundance and uses this abundance to create a more harmonious reality for themselves and others. The Spiritual Entrepreneur has confidence in themselves and believes in their gut that they are on the right path – and are not easily led astray. They do not measure themselves to others.

It is unwise to compare yourself to others. It is wise to focus on your own game and not your opponent's. Once you start thinking about how the other team is playing, you lose your focus. You become distracted and divided because consciously or unconsciously you start unwisely wanting to play the way the other team is playing. With the ability to compare comes the ability to judge – both yourself and others. The Spiritual Entrepreneur runs their own race. While everyone is going one way, they go in the opposite direction. They remind themselves daily of who they are, who they want to become and why they are here.

FROM SACRIFICE COMES MEANING; FROM STRUGGLE COMES PURPOSE

A little while back, after giving a keynote speech on 'Science, spirituality and entrepreneurship', a young man asked me what it takes to become an entrepreneur, and what I have had to sacrifice in order to achieve what I set out to achieve. I told him that to become a successful entrepreneur takes everything that you have – just as it does to become a successful speaker or writer or restaurateur or teacher or parent. I told him that he should only become an entrepreneur if he couldn't *not* be an entrepreneur. Elon Musk describes starting one's own company as 'like eating glass and staring into the abyss of death'. The entrepreneur's journey is ruthless because so many people want to become one.

To create something powerful and important you must at the very least be driven by an equally powerful inner force, because there is real pain and real pleasure either way. In the course of making the work, you are going to have to ask yourself, 'What am I willing to sacrifice in order to fulfil my purpose?' Significant sacrifice always lies in the heart of every great work. If it didn't, everyone would do it. To actually give something up in the pursuit of your work is not only necessary but also rewarding. When you know that you are destined for greatness, your potential haunts you. It keeps you up at night, and you won't feel complete until you manifest your higher purpose.

If we can romanticise any aspects about entrepreneurship, they are the single-minded determination, as well as the struggle and dedication acquired to get it right, and the motivating force that makes it all possible. These are the keys to lasting transformation. When we have a higher purpose, we possess the energy and the courage to continually venture outside of our comfort zone to get it done.

The size of our dreams must always exceed our current capacity to achieve them.

COGNITIVE DISSONANCE BECOMES OUR PREFERRED ART FORM

In the field of psychology, cognitive dissonance is the mental discomfort experienced by a person who simultaneously holds two or more contradictory beliefs, ideas or values. Some see this as a bad thing. I see it as a great thing! Cognitive dissonance allows for mental disruption – when you literally disrupt your own mind by thinking of yourself in a way that doesn't match your current behaviour. Cognitive dissonance is saying, 'I am absolutely petrified at public speaking, but I want to become a top keynote speaker' or 'I've never written a book before and am positively crap at writing, but I want to become an international bestselling author' or 'I am unfit and overweight right now, but I want to have a bitchin' body and world class health' or 'I have no idea where to start, but I want to open the most awarded Vietnamese restaurant in the world' or 'I will probably get laughed at, at first, but I want to help ease the personal suffering of many, and push forward humanity with my movement of Spiritual Entrepreneurs'.

The tension can be injected suddenly or allowed to build over time. And your mind says, 'Wait a minute … I don't know how to do these things! What do you mean? I have to actually practice speaking in front of thousands of people if I am to share my insights and tap into my greatest gifts?' or 'What? I'll have to be disciplined and unwavering in my commitment if I am to write a book?' or 'Seriously? I'll have to love myself if I am to be loved?' or 'Really? I'll have to treat my body responsibly if I'm to be fit and look fabulous?' or 'What do you mean? I have to work really hard to build a world class restaurant? This is big! Who do you think you are, Pauline? People will all laugh at you! This is scary stuff!'

Making a big life change is scary. But, you know what's even scarier? Regret. You have to get scared. You have to scare somebody, so why not scare yourself to be the best version of yourself? If you are serious about change, you have to go through uncomfortable situations. You can't dodge this process. It is the only way to grow. Your mind will be so uncomfortable with this dissonance that it will call on you to alter your attitudes, beliefs and behaviours so as to reduce the discomfort and match your desired behaviour.

Every creation begins as a thought. Astonishing science is behind how our brain creates our material reality. Our thoughts become things. When you think a thought, your mind is already poised to do it – poised and waiting for you to take action, to take the unmanifest to manifest. Once the door of awareness opens, you cannot close it. As soon as you truly commit to making something happen, the 'how' will reveal itself. Abundant thinkers constantly put themselves in cognitive dissonance.

All dreams come with built-in challenges, and all challenges come with built-in dreams. Overcome the challenges and live happier than you were before they arrived. Mike Dooley puts it beautifully, 'Challenges are not a sign of weakness, but of strength – evidence that a slumbering giant is about to awaken.'

DESIGNING YOUR POWERFUL PURPOSE STATEMENT

All the great entrepreneurial visionaries have their own Powerful Purpose Statement. If you are going to create great success in every area of your life, you will need one too. A purpose statement is four or five sentences, no more than a paragraph. It is a synthesis of your priorities and principles. It is a touchstone, a place to revisit daily that will help you to stay on point with your priorities and purpose. It is the North Star by which to navigate your life. When you can always see the big picture, and you are persistent in living in alignment with your highest values, you can create a meaningful, purposeful and fulfilling life for yourself, and continue to make a positive impact on the lives of others. This creates lasting happiness. This is true success.

Let's start with what your purpose statement is not. Your purpose statement is not to do with measuring anything externally. It is not to do with anything temporal, and it is not a goal. It is your own purposeful, powerful paragraph that is personal to you. It's your personal code of behaviour. It is an easy to understand written commitment to yourself of a daily way of being. It is both a declaration and an affirmation. It is a declaration of who you are and what you stand for. It is an affirmation of the way you want to respond and behave on those occasions when you lose your centre or forget who you are.

A purpose statement is something important to have in your back pocket and review daily because it instantly inspires and uplifts. It immediately brings you into harmony with your higher reason for being. It brings you back into alignment with your highest calling. It is the fountainhead, and the source from which all outer success springs forth.

If we don't have a purpose statement and review it regularly, we can easily become forgetful. We can fall prey to a lower frequency way of operating – meaning that we can find ourselves at the effect of negative energy. We can inadvertently allow ourselves to be at the mercy of the suboptimal thinking and behaviour of others and be thrown off our centre. If we get thrown off our centre, we become less effective in creating and experiencing the highest vision of our life.

Dolores Cannon, author, speaker and director of the Quantum Healing Hypnosis Academy, wrote that the main lesson we have come to Earth to learn is how to manipulate our energy. What this means is learning how to create your own reality and how to create the events in your life – in other words, how to become a master manifester. As Dolores said,

This is what a lot of people don't understand. There are no limitations except for the limitations you put on yourself. If you can visualise it in your mind, it is already done. That is the law of the universe. If you don't like what is happening in your life, you can change it and that's what it means about learning how to manipulate energy and change the events that you are experiencing. You have control over this, and the main thing to learn is how to do it – how to change your reality and create your reality. Everything in your life, you have put there, you have created. If you don't like what's happening in your life, you can change it. This is powerful information for people who think that they are stuck.

If we have a purpose statement and review it daily, we are in the top 1 per cent of human beings who are going about the business of consciously creating their life.

If you have a strong purpose in life, you don't have to be pushed. Your passion will drive you there. To the extent that we have control in this life, we are able to exercise that control, to harness and channel our energy in the most inspired and fulfilling way.

Here are the four secrets to designing your Powerful Purpose Statement:

1. *Limit it to a few sentences.* The statement should be one paragraph long as a maximum.

2. *Make it inspiring.* The statement must be a critical mission. It must be essential to the success of your life and your businesses.

3. *Write your statement in the present tense.* The Universe is a wish-granting machine. It will give you exactly what you ask for. You have to have an idea of what it is you want before you can create it. Whatever it is, you must visualise it and picture it because if you can see it in your mind, it is already done, it has already happened. This is the law of the Universe.

   Say something like, 'I want this,' or 'I need this' uses the wrong words. In creating your reality, if you say, 'I need' or 'I want', you are creating a lack and you are putting it off by wanting it.

The wording you must use is, 'I have' or 'I am' and you must believe it. There are the Laws of the Universe called the Law of Abundance and the Law of Attraction. You can have anything you want, once you know what it is and execute the action plan to achieve it.

4. *Make sure that your statement uses your seven personal principles.* I discussed your personal principles in the previous secret. Also include transcendental qualities – the qualities that are timeless and eternal. 'I am the top real estate agent in my country' is a good example of what not to write. Why? Because that statement is made in reference to others. Your purpose in life is less to do with where you rank in relationship to others and more to do where you rank in relationship with yourself.

Let's use the principles from the last secret as a foundation. These were:

- HEALTH
- LOVE
- INNER PEACE
- INFLUENCE
- SPIRITUAL
- INSPIRATION
- EVOLVE

Using these principles, I can create the following example statement:

I am healthy, fit and vital. I live under the aegis of grace, humour and humility. Every day, I fill my heart with gratitude, love, joy and inner peace. I view everything that happens in my life as a miracle. I am the alchemist of my life and the entire universe is conspiring in my favour. To inspire, uplift and elevate others to discover their own glorious potential is what I am put on this earth to do. I continually move into and share the next level of enlightenment. I leave everyone I meet with a sense of increase.

Your purpose or mission statement is the acorn that will grow into a massive oak tree. Living life without a unique Powerful Purpose Statement is like sailing a ship without a compass.

NEVER UNDERESTIMATE THE POWER OF A DECISION

Of all the people in this world, 98 per cent are spending 98 per cent of their time on the things that don't matter. This is also the reason so many people experience life the way it is. The Spiritual Entrepreneur prefers to focus their energy on the things that *do* matter. They live their life deliberately and not by default. They move ever forward in the process of becoming the fullest expression of their true nature. When you are the best version of yourself, you become fearless, and there can be no competition. Nobody can be a better me than me.

The quest of a Spiritual Entrepreneur is the same as all seekers around the world – to discover those elements that align your actions with your purpose, allowing you to experience the flow and the glorious beauty of life.

When your vision becomes your mission, your business will become a movement. Spiritual Entrepreneurship is about discovering your gifts, actualising your gifts and sharing these with the world. The key to purpose is using your strengths to serve others.

If you don't pursue the challenges that inspire you, you will fill your days with the challengers who don't. Bruce Lee once said, 'We should devote ourselves to being self-sufficient and must not depend upon the external ratings by others for our happiness.' In business as in life, you cannot strive to be better than the competition; you must strive to be different from the competition.

A Gallup study found that the number one reason people worked long into their 90s was not because they were happy with their jobs. Yes, they were happy, but the number one reason was that their jobs gave their lives meaning. They all felt that what they were doing was their purpose and that they were contributing to the world. Health deteriorates rapidly for those who lose touch with their purpose. The alignment of your work with your core values is the key to fulfilment and lasting happiness. It contributes to being present and gives meaning to life. Living your life's mission is the key to longevity. Why? Because when we can truly internalise this, we can eliminate stress, uncertainty and worry. My Awaken the Spiritual Entrepreneur program assists overwhelmed professionals and individuals from all walks of life to tap into new levels of abundance and live their life purpose in powerful ways.

Every entrepreneur knows that the success of their businesses ultimately rests on their shoulders. Yes, the product you build and the team you hire are important, but your ability to lead is what carries your companies to success. The Spiritual Entrepreneur who lives their purpose does not have to chase people or opportunities. Their light and their energy cause people and opportunities to pursue them. When you live on purpose, and in purpose, people won't be able to take their eyes off you. People want to see a thing of beauty, and of courage, and of ego-free swagger. The ones who are ready will follow you and hang off every word you say. They will want to see you and watch you over and over again, and shine in the light of your own greatness.

The effect we have on others is the most valuable currency we have.

Live on purpose.

Be a contagion.

'The Way' Secret #4

UNLEARN EVERYTHING – REDESIGN YOUR DESTINY

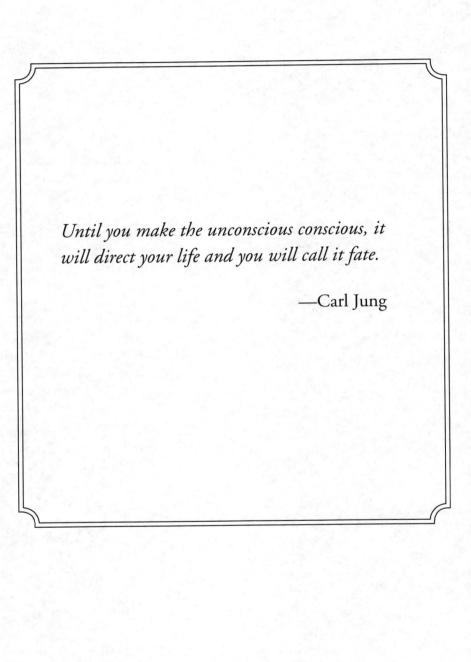

Until you make the unconscious conscious, it will direct your life and you will call it fate.

—Carl Jung

CHANGING YOUR GUIDANCE SYSTEM

Remember – personal development cannot happen unless personal disruption happens first.

Change your story and you will change your life. One of the concepts I have been researching in recent years is a concept called 'family constellations'. Also known as 'systemic family constellations', this is the idea that, while we may think of ourselves as separate from each other, we are, of course, connected. We are connected, in particular, to our lineage – to our family – and we tend to unconsciously play out our family's patterns. We unconsciously repeat these patterns over and over. In constellation work, the lineage is powerful. It reveals an unrecognised systemic dynamic that spans multiple generations in a given family. Practitioners claim that present-day problems and difficulties may be influenced by traumas suffered in previous generations of the family, even if those affected now are unaware of the original event in the past.

We have had beliefs that have been handed down to us from generation to generation. Those beliefs are usually designed to protect us and give us a guidance system to go through life with. It is our ancestors trying to hand down their wisdom and guidance to us. And yet, in the last 150 years, the world has changed so radically that we really have to question whether that guidance system is still serving us. It is important to question everything. It is important that we challenge our existing paradigms and transcend the status quo. It is important to question the beliefs that no longer make sense and no longer serve us. It is important to question the beliefs that cause us pain.

Well-known idioms such as 'Money doesn't grow on trees' or 'Money is the root of all evil' or 'You must work hard for the money' are examples of beliefs handed down to us. They are loaded statements that tell us that we live in a world of lack and that there is not much to go around. These beliefs are intended to serve us; however, the reality is they are not serving us to the degree that they could. Most people have a strong desire and dream for a better life. The natural order by which we live gives us abundant opportunities for a better life, and yet the belief system that we've inherited from previous generations holds us back.

In my work, I get to assist people from all walks of life, and I know that one thing is for certain. I know that many of you reading these pages have followed the path that your parents and your families have set out for you. You have done what your culture and your society has told you to do. And you are likely deeply unhappy and feel trapped – you are not free. I know, because I was one of you. I also know that many of us feel a deeper truth. There is a deeper knowing in our hearts. There is a sense of, 'This relationship isn't right. I'm not happy.' Or a sense of, 'This job isn't in alignment with my highest purpose. I am compromising who I am.' Or a sense of, 'Why am I here with these so-called friends? They do not bring out the best in me. They do not inspire or uplift me.' But we are often afraid. There is a deep-seated fear that we are not even aware of. And the fear lies so deep that when life comes knocking at our door with all its challenges and all its confrontations, we slowly start to shut down and we start learning a whole new way of being because we are afraid to feel. We do our best to avoid pain, to disconnect, to not be loved, and to ultimately just exist ... to simply survive ... and so, we numb ourselves to life.

Rediscovering your true essence

This is how this progression towards numbness works. As children, we are born free. We are born to be great. We are born into genius. We are born to shine. We are born to win. As children, we are born in touch with the sense of aliveness and joy. We didn't care what people thought about us. We did what we wanted to do. When we were kids, all we did was play. We literally did what we loved to do. Drawing, singing, dancing, role playing all day. We played and we created. We played all day and pretended we were the people we wanted to be when we grew up. We started adopting early, the skills of imagination, creation, collaboration and fantasy which assists in building healthy self esteem. We could look at our reflection in the mirror and only see beauty, power and perfection. We were complete, whole, significant, purposeful, connected and present. Up until age four, our brain waves were functioning in delta – we were operating at a genius level. Our creativity was what was running us. Our energy was running from the inside out.

When you were a child, you were busy working on YOU. You were working on you and excelling at that. And because of that, you were undeniably amazing. This same mentality exists in all the people who are the greatest at what they do. A child will dance and laugh and love freely. A child will throw their arms around you and kiss you all over. A child will come up to you and say, 'Hi! Can I tickle you?' They won't care if you are black, white or yellow. A child expresses freely. They are in touch with their true essence. That is why when we look into a child's eyes, we are reminded of who we really are. The child connects us to ourselves.

But then something happened. The adults in our life happened. Our parents happened. Culture happened. Five minutes after your birth, they decide your name, your nationality and your religion. So, along with the milk and baby food, our parents, our families and our teachers subconsciously feed us a daily diet of obedience, compliance and how to be. They feed us their beliefs, their rules, their limitations, their values and their prejudices. All of this gets downloaded onto us and, unwittingly, we set off on the conveyor belt of the system we call childhood.

And as we went through life, we were taught to lose. We slowly lost touch with our true nature and our true essence. And then we had to deal with our parents – most of whom had no idea what they were doing. There is no such thing as 'Parent University' is there? And we were told what to do, and we were scolded and yelled at: 'Behave yourself!', 'Don't be silly!', 'Don't be stupid!', 'You can't do that!', 'Stop crying!', 'Stop talking!', 'Stop laughing!', 'Stop mucking around!' 'STOP! Just STOP!' We are buried in a society that tells us, 'No.' 'Behave.' 'Follow the rules.' 'You can't do this.' By the time a child reaches 17 years of age, they have heard 'No' one hundred and fifty thousand times and 'Yes' only five thousand times.

And so, we dim our light and we stop. We do what we are told because we want to be loved. We want to be accepted. We want Mum and

Dad to not be angry at us. We learn quickly that we can't do stuff. Every decision we make now is based on what other people think about us, and we feel incomplete without the external validation. We are now affected from the outside in.

And then we slowly start losing touch with that essential nature, that divinity, that infinity, that spark, the true essence of who we are. So, our parents' beliefs become our beliefs. Society's rules become our rules. Our culture's values become our values, and we grow up defending these beliefs, rules and values as if they were our own. We believe what we are told and we spend the rest of our life defending something we didn't even choose. Some defend these beliefs until the death even when new discoveries tell us the stories are wrong. Our psychology becomes a symptom of our self-image – the self-esteem that was set by our parents.

Clinical psychologist Dr Shefali Tsabary calls this 'spirit abduction', telling us,

> *You were told you are lesser than, and you have to become and do, do, do. Accomplish, fit in, belong, accommodate, please. In other words, stop who you authentically are. And slowly, imperceptibly sometimes, but surely layer by layer, who you essentially were was stripped off from you. Piece by piece your selfhood was slivered into pieces left strewn on the sidewalk of your childhood. But you're obedient, naive, innocent. We trust our parents. We believe our culture. Looking back at childhood, we realize we each had that 'something' that we so badly seek as adults. We trusted our significance, we had immeasurable wonder, and we were fully present in each moment. We were overflowing with our authentic spirit. But then, we lost it, as we strived to become worthy, to meet other people's standards, to check off all the boxes of what's supposed to make us happy only to realize we feel incomplete and empty.*

We run around all day hoping and wishing on external factors. And this is why many are in fear. Have you ever stopped to question how much of what we believe is because we have always believed it, based on what someone else has taught us, or from a religious construct, doctrine or theology? How much is derived from or influenced by our particular culture and society? If you are under the illusion that these things outside of you are what complete you, you will always be a victim because everything has to change to make you happy.

How exhausting! How overwhelmingly exhausting it is to walk this earth being someone you are not! We need to come to terms with the true cost of this. For most, it is not until our thirties – or, for some of us, much later in life – that we wake up a little and start realising that we have been sleepwalking. We start to question a little; we might start to say, 'Wait a minute, no-one ever asked my permission to dump their beliefs on me. This is not okay. This is not working for me. I am my own separate person. I can think for myself and this does not feel good. This does not feel right.' And then we wake up a little more, and we tap into the part of us that is no longer happy with how things are. We snatch back our power, and we realise that we are not helpless. We realise that we can unlearn a lot of the untruths that were taught to us by people who didn't know what they were doing either. And then we wake up a little more, and we have the courage to question e-v-e-r-y-t-h-i-n-g.

The unexamined life is not worth living. —Socrates

I am a proponent of constantly analysing my own beliefs. When I first started to question what my environment and my culture had previously told me, I found that the beliefs that had been handed down to me were outdated and archaic. The beliefs I had gathered from my surroundings and my family about who and what I was were in no way benefitting me in my life. I now limit my beliefs to my own experiences. My experience is really the only thing that I know. Unless I have had direct experience, I will continue the questioning process. Does the belief make sense? Does the belief serve me in my life? If I have experienced something directly, then I have some real information about the experience and I can teach from an authentic space. Analysing the beliefs is where the process starts. We must put in the work. This can be difficult for many people. But it is not about 'the work' – it's about who you become in the process of being committed to doing the work. Ask yourself the important questions: 'Why am I here? Who am I? What do I want?'

Rather than stating, 'My belief is …' try saying, 'My current belief is …'

BETTER A MIND OPENED BY WONDER THAN ONE CLOSED BY BELIEF

What are beliefs? Beliefs are the blueprint we use to build the structure of our existence and create our reality. But do you know what beliefs really are? Beliefs are habits – habits that you have practised all your life, or new habits that you have adopted along the way. We all know that habits can be broken, right? And we all know that new habits can be formed. I challenge you to break the habits that are not serving you. I challenge you to break the habits that are causing you pain. If the beliefs downloaded by your culture have caused wars, conflict, abuse and killing, then forgive those who fed you the destructive beliefs, for they know not what they do. They know not what they do because they know not who they are.

If you are still attached to your religion, your colour or the country you were born in, you still do not know who and what you truly are, and what you are truly capable of. If you do not know the deepest truths of your existence as you are exposed to new cultures, new religions and new beliefs, you will always feel threatened.

I encourage you to adopt new habits – the new habits that bring you more joy and more peace; the habits that will make your heart sing. We need to stop and question everything that has been taught to us. It takes but sixty-six days for a habit to be successfully broken and a new habit to be formed. You cannot build a fulfilling future if you have not worked through the burdens of your past. Finding yourself consists of peeling off the years of social conditioning to find a self as it existed during childhood, unmasked. You must unlearn what you have been programmed to believe since birth. That software no longer serves you if you want to live in a world where all things are possible.

To remember who you are, you need to forget who they told you to be.

The Spiritual Entrepreneur is continually learning new concepts and installing new belief systems. They understand that it is their responsibility to expand their mind, and to continually grow and evolve. Because the more they learn, the more they learn that there is always more to learn. The Spiritual Entrepreneur reinvents themselves continually. They become a completely different person on a regular basis to upgrade their character, their habits and their beliefs – because who they used to be is not capable of doing what they want to achieve.

HOW DO YOU CHANGE A BELIEF?

Of all of the beautiful truths pertaining to the soul which have been restored and brought to light in this age, none is more gladdening and fruitful of divine promise and confidence than this – that you are the master of your thought, the moulder of your character, and the maker and shaper of condition, environment and destiny. —James Allen

People respect what you inspect. Digging into and interrogating your beliefs about abundance and success are key to making sure that you can achieve the life that you really want. A friend once said to me, 'Consider how hard it is to change yourself and you'll understand what little chance you have in changing others.' My friend's comment follows the common view that change is difficult. I disagree wholeheartedly. The first concept to get a grasp of – and truly get a grasp of – is this: CHANGE IS INCREDIBLY EASY! So much so that we are designed to do it without even thinking. Change, growth, progress – however you wish to term it, it is the very reason for our existence.

Our purpose on this earth is to change. So much so that our species is designed to change without us even trying. Think about it – our hair, our fingernails, our skin, our facial features, our bodies, our internal organs, our sexual organs, our external limbs … all of it, changes and grows and morphs without us even thinking. Our body is constantly renewing itself. Miraculously, while every cell in your body ages and eventually dies, ten to twenty million cells are dying and being replaced by new cells every second. Homo sapiens are here to change and grow.

Change is the only constant. In business, as in life, we must not only embrace change, but also learn to expect change. Not only must we expect change, but we must also learn to be-the-change. All great change is preceded by chaos.

To start the process of change, we must start by deleting all the old stories that no longer serve us. The stories we tell ourselves about ourselves and believe define our lives. For many years, I allowed my childhood memories to run my life. The childhood experiences that triggered strong emotions had a massive influence on the beliefs that I created about the world around me. These beliefs resurfaced in my daily life as an adult with damaging results. I let the stories define who I was. The unwanted patterns repeated over and over and made me feel helpless and out of control. I did not want this to be my fate. Unless the old stories can be retold in the service of others as a tool to impart wisdom, we must stop retelling and reliving the same stories over and over. The possibility lives in our heart, not in our head.

Science tells us that only 50 per cent of the old stories we tell ourselves and others are true. Why? Because we tell them through different lenses every time. How? Because we are constantly changing and becoming new people. We are literally a different person each time we tell the story. The story is no longer true. When an event or incident has an emotion attached to it, it becomes a memory. Change the emotion attached to it and the memory will change. When we can share a memory without the emotional charge, it becomes wisdom. When this happens, it is no longer called change, it is called evolution.

IT IS NEVER TOO LATE TO HAVE HAD A HAPPY CHILDHOOD

Growing up, I witnessed all the anger, fear and trauma in my father, along with all the emotional toxicity that had built up in him over the years. His own father was also a violent man who passed on his anger to my father. I come from a family of resistance fighters who fought for freedom and liberation at all cost. It is my lineage. And once I started to examine my own past, I realised my true self was conscious enough to make the decision that the cycle must end with me. I did not want to pass on my anger and trauma to the next generation. There are lessons from my parents' lives that are positive. Everything they went through in coming to Australia reflects the values and the truth of my life now: calm courage, resilience and grit. My parents possessed such courage to take massive action and escape into unknown waters. They possessed unwavering resilience – the ability to fall and get back up again and again. And they possessed true grit – the stamina and determination to achieve their long-term goals in the face of adversity.

My father did the best he could with the tools that he had at the time. He lives a different life now, and we are friends. Just as he had a choice, so too do I have a choice. We all get to choose.

Pain is inevitable; suffering is a choice

Not having the freedom to let go leads to a miserable existence. That is not to say that we should close our eyes and ears, or ignore the relative logic of life. But what is important is how we translate and interpret what happens. Because we all have a choice. I work with so many people who have been unable to choose the story that gives them peace, so they take a painful event, put more lenses and more filters on it, until it becomes misery and they suffer needlessly and endlessly. This absence of consciousness causes people to suffer because of the stories they have created and the layers of meaning they have piled onto those stories. All of this becomes a rock that they are chained to.

Every emotion has energy. How can you become iconic in business and in life when you are weighed down with toxic emotion? When you are heartbroken and discouraged? When you have guilt and rage running through your veins that you do not acknowledge? Most people are unconscious of the toxicity. The missing link is to work through the emotional toxin.

Change your story and you will change your life

In her book *The Abundance Code*, Julie Ann Cairns writes that, after working with and teaching many hundreds of clients to trade in the financial markets, she discovered a set of seven limiting beliefs about money, success and abundance that most people have that are holding them back. And if you can eliminate those beliefs, then that's 80 or 90 per cent of the battle. Cairns also discovered a common three-step framework that must be followed if we are to change our limiting beliefs.

The first step is to identify your top seven limiting beliefs. This is the hardest step because our beliefs are subconscious. They are below the level of our conscious awareness. Most of our behaviours, decisions and actions are guided with our unconscious/subconscious mind – the part of the mind that you cannot consciously access. I prefer to call it the 'non-conscious' mind. To give it the prefix of 'sub' understates the power that it truly holds.

The only way to see what is locked away in our mind's archive is to monitor our behaviours over time. We need to look out for discrepancies and incongruences in what we say we are going to do and what we actually do. The discrepancies between our words and our behaviours will give a window into our non-conscious mind so that we can identify what lies beneath the surface. And what you will discover is that the cause of events and your actions wasn't fate after all, and it was you all along. And once you are aware of this, the non-conscious suddenly becomes conscious – and this is where change happens.

The second step to belief change is to weaken the existing limiting belief. This is an important step that a lot of people miss. When you don't weaken the limiting belief first, it is hard to put a new belief on top of it and have it succeed. This is where an effective coach or mentor can assist by going through each belief and presenting current data and evidence from a strong research background, and combining this with skilful encouragement. Arguing the counter-case weakens the hold of that belief in your mind. In business and in life, challenging beliefs is 50 per cent tactical or logical and 50 per cent mental or psychological. The obstacle blocking most people is never material;

it is imaginary, and it is a delusion of belief systems that has been created in the participant's mind, passed on by external influences.

And the third step is the easiest step. It is where you replace that old limiting belief with a belief that isn't going to limit you. This is where tools such as vision boards, meditations, visualisation, hypnosis, NLP, or a skilful coach and mentor can accelerate the process and help you achieve rapid results in opening up a new belief. The coach or mentor can burst the bubbles of delusion to help you to see things clearly and teach the tactical/logical things necessary to succeed in business and in life. They can help you to discover what is hiding in your non-conscious and make it conscious so you can change – because until somebody can see, the tactical weapons are useless. A skilful coach or mentor doesn't fix the problem for you. They help to elevate your thinking so that the problem fixes itself. This is true self-sustainability.

From awareness stems change

True freedom comes when we are defined by a vision of the future, and are no longer held hostage by the painful memories of our childhood and the emotional bondage of the past.

The starting point of all achievement is desire. Keep this constantly in mind. Weak desires bring weak results. Ask yourself, 'What if there was another way?' 'What if I were called to live another life?' 'What if the destiny and the divinity in me was to have it all?' It takes an enormous amount of courage to question your existing paradigms and think that you might not be right. It takes an enormous amount of courage to admit that the way you see the world might be flawed in some way or that there may be a better way of thinking or behaving or living. It takes an enormous amount of courage to open your mind and your heart. In her work, Cairns realised that the psychology of her clients was a symptom of their self-image – an image that had been passed down to them by their parents, culture and environment.

As a Spiritual Entrepreneur, being vulnerable is about knowing yourself so intimately that you have a secure sense of self-identity. As a leader, this starts with a deep reflective intimacy with owning who you are. It is shedding the masks and veneers of who you think you are or who you think you need to be in order to be successful. Running away from uncertainty, uncomfortable feelings or situations that frighten you won't keep you safe. What you are really doing is running away from your growth. Feeling uncomfortable is often the first stage of growth. What you are avoiding and running away from will ultimately continue to come back around in another disguise until you finally 'get it' and apply it in your own life. Hold yourself accountable for facing your fears, for choosing what happens next, for facing the lesson and uncovering the blessing that is hidden within it.

People who feel good about themselves do great work

The best version of you will lead the best version of your people. We become excellent by doing excellent things. Over and over we must do excellent things. Every time you practice a weakness you feed it and the things you feed grow in your life. We become fearless by continually visiting the places that scare us. We become strong by living our strengths, not our weakness. The only person you are destined to become is who you decide to be. Who will you decide to be?

Now that you know how to change your beliefs and rewrite your narrative, the next step is to discover a professional mission that allows you to express your unique gifts and talents that are in harmony with your personal principles.

DISCOVERING YOUR PROFESSIONAL MISSION

Your work is going to fill a large part of your life, and the only way to be truly satisfied is to do what you believe is great work. And the only way to do great work is to love what you do. If you haven't found it yet, keep looking. Don't settle. —Steve Jobs

As a Spiritual Entrepreneur, it is important to make sure that your day-to-day professional life is in orbit around your life principles, and not the other way around.

Having a vision and knowing what you are here to do shows up in your body, and your job is to lock onto it tight. And when you do, you become safe from all the people who start to judge the new you. A lot of people will not see your vision and will not accept your new deliberate self. The old world will remind you of your old story and try to convince you that 'This is who you are. This is your fate.' They will look at life based on how they have, and you have, always done things so far. They will rehash the stories of old and share with you their limiting beliefs. They will remind you of the old paradigm that you are not supposed to love your work, and that's why they call it work. They will doubt you and tell you that your current circumstances do not fit in with your new vision.

This is when you need to tap into that part of you that is no longer happy with how things are. This is when you snatch back your power. You are not helpless. Tap into that part of you that continues to show up when everyone else around you disappears or crumbles. When everyone else around you gives up. When everyone else around you doubts and questions whether you can pull it off. There is a switch inside you, deep down inside – in business, in relationships, in life – that says, 'Fuck this. I will get it done no matter what!'

Way back in the 16th century, Niccolò Machiavelli told us,

> *It should be borne in mind that there is nothing more difficult to handle, or more doubtful of success and more dangerous to carry through than initiating changes … The innovator makes enemies of all those who prospered under the old order and receives only lukewarm support from those who would prosper under the new.*

Remember that, at every turn, the truer you are to yourself and the more you live in congruence, the more fulfilled you will be and the more lasting is your happiness. You must keep a high happiness score to get to and stay in Quadrant 4. Defy the odds. Set a new standard for yourself. Never fall into the trap of sacrificing or compromising your core principles in the now, based on the stories of the past or the possibility of some imagined gain in the future that is incongruent with who you truly are. When people start judging you and doubting you, you have the opportunity to hold onto your vision tighter and start doing what the vision calls for. And through the process, you start to ignore the current circumstances and, instead, you will create your new reality – not one based on the current circumstances, but one based on what your vision is.

Here's what I mean. If, for example, one of your core principles is love and connection and you are offered a solo job as a light-house operator on a remote island, your income might go up, but your happiness score will go down. Remember that the Spiritual Entrepreneur in Quadrant 4 has, by definition, happiness and wealth. But we must get the happy part down first! In previous chapters, we have redefined what lasting happiness is – it is not 'positive thinking' and being happy '24/7'. Lasting happiness is living as your authentic self and experiencing fulfilment by doing what you love. Happiness is about discovery and listening to your heart. Happiness is about being kinder to yourself and finding your joy and embracing the person you are becoming. Happiness is about learning how to live with yourself. Your happiness was never in the hands of other people.

Life shrinks or expands according to one's courage. —Anaïs Nin

Love what you do; do what you love

Discovering your life's calling or mission is finding your purpose and doing work that you love. When you have a vision and you ignore the circumstances, the circumstances end up moulding around your vision. When you hold onto that vision and ignore how the world currently works, your circumstances become the vision, and you uncover who you really are. Some people risk their life for money. What if you risk money for life? If you have a job that you need to retire from, maybe it's not your calling. Maybe you're here to do what you love so much that you'll die doing it.

Getting in sync with your professional mission in life means two things. The first is that you are working on something where 'your reason for being and doing' extends beyond yourself to contribute to and elevate the greater whole. The second is that you are passionate and energised every day about what you do. The action itself is a form of compensation. Of course, you will get paid, but your attention is captured not by the money, but by the joy of doing what you love.

A well-known non-commercial example is Mother Teresa. She was on a mission to care for people in the slums of India and became world famous for it. Commercial examples include Sir Richard Branson and, of course, the late Steve Jobs. When we discover our mission and commit to it, we unleash a tremendous amount of energy. The Universe affords us this energy, because the mission is about not only our own personal fulfilment but also the fulfilment of others. When your purpose is bigger than your individuality and tied into the service of humanity, an ocean of potential energy is made available to you. Outsiders may be astounded, as you appear on your own to be doing the work of many.

When you are on a mission, one that is naturally aligned with your personal principles, you will be able to work extraordinary hours and not feel like you are working. You will be able to build a career where every day can feel like a vacation because you love the work you do. You will inspire and uplift others and have to ability to claim your Quadrant 4 heritage.

Keep in mind that as much as you hope to find your professional mission, your mission is searching to find you.

How do you know if you have found your professional mission? Nature communicates that you are moving in the right direction in life through the inner sensation of inspiration. You will feel alive and with a level of energy you have never felt before. You will know what it means to be 'in-spirit'. You will experience the height of your 'spirituality.' There is a potent magic in the mysterious nature of inspiration. When you are pursuing your professional mission and living according to your highest values wholeheartedly, you have complete access to your physical, mental and spiritual resources.

If what you are doing feels inspiring, you know you are on point and heading in the right direction. Your world will crack open with wonder and joy. I seldom feel like I am working hard. The international speaking engagements, the intense travel schedule, the workshops, the retreats, the webinars, the writing, the meetings, the collaborations, the restaurant work – they do not seem like hard work. My life is inspiring and fulfilling because I love what I do and I do what I love. I set my goals and intentions accordingly. On the other hand, if you consistently feel uncomfortable or have an aversion to a job or a situation, it is nature's way of communicating that what you are doing is not the right fit for you. You are probably heading in the wrong direction and a course correction is needed.

Higher life designers do not need motivation. They seek inspiration for transformation. They tap into their internal inspiration and transform by choice. Their strong sense of 'Why' enables them to discover a plethora of 'Hows'. When you discover work you love, you can also rest assured that what you are doing is helping not only you, but also those around you. You can be sure that you are offering a positive contribution to society – not doing harm. It would be extremely unlikely that a bank robber or a handgun smuggler would go to their job with a skip in their step. 'I am so happy and inspired by my job of robbing banks and smuggling guns.' Unlikely. It is difficult to find happiness and the sense that we are on purpose through actions, whether professional or otherwise, where we potentially hurt or do harm to others. Incidentally, it is only unhappy people who commit crimes.

Locking in on your mission

If you desire to live the Way of Spiritual Entrepreneur and access Quadrant 4 success, it is essential to discover your mission because your time here is finite. It is the most precious thing you have. You don't want to spend a second wasting your energy in situations that bring you anything less than complete satisfaction and fulfilment. It is essential to discover your professional mission because it will require nothing less to create monumental success in your chosen field. It is difficult to fulfil your entrepreneurial potential unless you discover and do work that you are passionate about. Great success requires 100 per cent commitment. It is impossible to give something your best if you feel half-hearted. That is why your professional mission must be an extension of your personal principles.

Here are three simple ways to figure out your professional mission:

1. Ask yourself the following questions. What pulls you? What compels you? What intrigues you? What excites you? What are your hobbies? Make time to do the things that elevate your soul. Time comes to those who make it, not to those who try to find it. Ask yourself, what makes your heart sing? What are you talented at? What are you good at? If you don't know, ask your closest friends or your closest family members. They can tell you what your talents are. Write down all the things that you enjoy. What you enjoy is closely linked to your talent.

2. Once you've noted your talents and hobbies, make another list of all the different professions you can think of that are connected to those talents and hobbies. This can help you hone in on your passion. To achieve a high level of expertise in anything, you have to do it a lot, and you're not going to do something a lot unless you enjoy it. And then when you enjoy it and you're doing it all the time, it's not work, it's a passion. And over time, through many years of spending time on that passion, you develop an expertise that comes with it, and it becomes the fullest expression of your true nature.

3. Ask yourself this question. 'What would I do if I won $100 million?' Believe it or not, you will get bored travelling the world first class after a few short years. You will be looking for an avenue through which to offer your innate gifts and talents. What would you do?

A business that is not continuously examined and re-examined is a business not worth owning. —Jay Abraham

If you are already doing work you love and have found your mission, that is a beautiful thing and I am happy for you. Now it's about constant fine-tuning. Within your various roles, what are the things you most enjoy? Do more of those things. For the tasks you don't enjoy, delegate them. Are you the administrator of your business or the leader of your business? As the leader of your organisation, you must delegate as much as possible so that you can be as free as possible to discover and rediscover your true professional mission. This is an ever-evolving process as you continue to interrogate, redefine and redesign yourself.

People will tell you that you are out of your mind. Stay with it. I encourage you to get out of your mind because the biggest callings do not show up in your head — they show up in your heart. So get out of your mind, stay with the vision, trust it and watch how the world will form and mould around you. When you listen to your vision and you live your genius, you become the visionary. Your dogged determination and unwavering internal certainty will elevate the people around you and inspire them.

VISIONARIES SEE THINGS DIFFERENTLY

In 2007, frustrated with the existing opportunities to fully express their passion, New York spin instructors Julie Rice and Elizabeth Cutler started a stationary bike studio on Manhattan's upper west side, calling it Soul Cycle. Rice and Cutler wanted to inject some spirit and soul into spinning, and created a class that included inspirational coaching, mind/body exercises and high-energy music. The first studio was a sublease within an existing space. Their offering was so popular that within five years they expanded to fourteen locations. In 2013 US sports club Equinox bought a percentage of Soul Cycle for a reported $25 million.

Dr Seuss's first book was rejected more than twenty times. He was on his way to burn the pages when he ran into a college friend who had recently been made children's editor at Vanguard Press. Seuss later said, 'If I'd been going down the other side of Madison Avenue, I'd be in the dry-cleaning business today.'

Gone with the Wind was rejected by thirty-eight publishers. Walt Disney was turned down three hundred and two times before finally getting financing for his dream of creating Walt Disney World. KFC founder Colonel Sanders was rejected one thousand and nine times before finding a taker for his chicken recipe. JK Rowling was rejected by twelve publishers before she was catapulted from her tiny Edinburgh apartment to worldwide recognition.

The Universe rewards the unreasonably determined

Finding your purpose and working from passion is not only inspiring but it will also translate to the bottom line. Imagine two versions of you, A and B. A is inspired and happy, operating on purpose with a mission to offer something great to the world. B is not so happy or inspired and is without a mission beyond surviving and maybe growing in business. It would be fair to say that A will soar beyond B in absolutely every objectively measurable criterion. A will work and it will be effortless.

A level of effortlessness comes through you enjoying the process of living your professional mission. Is that not what our life's goals should be about? And when you succeed in living your professional mission, the results will show up when they are supposed to. Let go of the results. Make your intention, let go of any desired results, and watch how quickly even better results show up. The wonderful piece of grace is that we are not alone in this Universe and something is helping us along our journey. Practising your professional mission and practising your craft in expert fashion is noble, honourable and satisfying. Humility in the pursuit of passion will never fail you.

Through my work, I assist many entrepreneurs to rewrite their narrative and choose the story that gives them the most peace, and to choose the thoughts that bring them the most joy. This is my professional mission – to change perspectives, to relieve suffering and create more opportunities in people's lives. I love to challenge and change perspectives. Not everybody is ready, which I respect. I believe I was put on this earth to influence people to design a life on their own terms, regardless of what they have been through. When we make that decision, even more joy, more gratitude, more inner peace and more adventure and beauty come our way – because our truth is not in being burdened by the anger, fear and trauma of the past. Gratitude begets gratitude. Abundance begets abundance. Love begets love. We all get to choose. This is true freedom.

> *Don't let the noise of others' opinions drown out your own inner voice. And most important, have the courage to follow your heart and intuition. They somehow already know what you truly want to become. Everything else is secondary.* —Steve Jobs

Regain your authentic spirit

Regaining our spirit allows us to awaken to who we truly are. We all inherently want to find a deep connection with ourselves and with others and reclaim our purpose for being here. Understanding that we had that 'something', that authentic spirit, so freely and naturally at one point in time is the first step towards getting it back. The better we know ourselves, the better equipped we are to overcome whatever adversity life throws our way. It is this simple fact that lies at the core of my Awaken the Spiritual Entrepreneur program, where I share the discoveries and techniques that leave no doubt that you are much more than you have been led to believe, and even beyond what you have imagined in the past. I have designed this program with you in mind, to zero in on your outdated beliefs and quash them so as to make room for who and what you truly are.

And when you uncover your true power, you will learn to speak your truth no matter how scary. Every negative pattern or belief will be transformed. You will learn to surrender to divine timing – which has nothing to do with your timing. At times it will hurt so much that you think you will die. But this is when you remind yourself of who you are, who you are becoming and why you are here. You will remind yourself of your mission and your soul agreement. You will understand that you are what you love and not what loves you. And this is the day you will become a true Spiritual Entrepreneur. When you know that no matter how dark it can get inside and outside, nothing will stop you and your mission – because you have already lived through that, and you have survived. And that was your training.

Our background and circumstances may influence who we are, but we are responsible for who we become. We must unlearn everything. We must redesign our destiny and choose our own adventure. The only person we are destined to become is the person we decide to be. Have the courage to redefine your life on your own terms. Because the place that you are used to is not where you belong.

‘The Way’ Secret #5

KNOW THYSELF, HEAL THYSELF, LOVE THYSELF

There is nothing outside of yourself that can ever enable you to get better, stronger, richer, quicker or smarter. Everything is within. Everything exists. Seek nothing outside of yourself.

—Miyamoto Musashi, *The Book of Five Rings*

THE POWER TO HEAL RESIDES IN US ALL

The mystery of nightfall comforted me. The evening was warm and I caught myself humming the old song of spring as I looked out the glass doors to my garden. I closed my eyes and wondered if the crickets were chirping the same song. The knock at the front door startled me. It was 9 pm on a Tuesday.

'Hey lady, what's up?' I motioned for Sarah to come in.

My friend pushed pass quickly and blurted her words. 'Good, you're home. I wanted to tell you in person.' The sweet scent of vanilla and rose water followed her and, as always, her clothes looked soft and expensive. She headed straight to my wine cabinet and poured us each a glass of pinot noir. I liked that she felt comfortable enough in my home to help herself to my things.

Let me backtrack a little. Sarah and I used to belong to the same entrepreneurs' mastermind group from which I left a short year later. While the mechanics of the mastermind group provided us with the 'nuts and bolts' advice of running a business, it did little to address and offer support for the real pain of being an entrepreneur – the deeper struggles that few are willing to admit and speak about. Sometimes, the groups burst at the seams with inflated egos and machismo. I did not belong, but Sarah hadn't understood why I'd wanted to leave. To her, the group represented 'success'. She once said to me, 'Only eagles understand eagles. Here, I get to fly with eagles.' I smiled and responded, 'Yes, but some eagles prefer to soar higher so that they can breathe in the rare air of truth and nonconformity.' She had no idea what I was on about at the time.

A few months after my departure from the group, Sarah had first reached out.

'Can I meet with you please? It's been a while. I need to be in your orbit. I need your help.'

'Sure,' I said. 'We can have dinner at Red Lantern if you like, I happen to know the owners.' Sarah was a high achiever and incredibly motivated to make a difference to the world. She co-owned a successful buyer's agency and had a strong vision of how she wanted her life to be. The advice shared in the mastermind group allowed her business to grow significantly year upon year. Within the entrepreneurial community, Sarah was considered a success in every way. She had a handsome husband, three kids, a great figure, several fancy cars, a media profile and a beautiful heart. Sarah acted upbeat, confident and quirky in front of most people. To only a few, she shared her vulnerable side. To me, she revealed the depth of her despair.

When Sarah joined me at Red Lantern, uneasiness enveloped us. My friend did not look well. The lethargy in her voice made me nervous. The erratic rhythm of her breath made me pay attention. Her forced smile made me sad. The smell of sickness permeated my nostrils as she drew closer and I could feel frailty through her white silk blouse when we embraced. She quietly acknowledged my silent surprise.

'The doctors tell me I'm dying.' She was never one for small talk. I liked that about her. I took a deep breath and nodded calmly in recognition. 'What can I do to help?'

'I'm sick. My body is fucked. The pain, the inflammation, the itching, the fatigue ... it's chronic. It's all fucking chronic. You thought my depression was bad? Try getting lupus on top of that!'

She unbuttoned two shirt buttons and gently pulled aside her long blonde locks to reveal weeping sores all over her chest caused by her malfunctioning immune system. She covered up quickly when our waiter arrived with mineral water. With shaking hands, she lifted the glass to her mouth and skulled all of it. 'Some days my bowels are so shot, I'm chained to the toilet seat wanting to kill myself.' She faked a laugh and continued. 'The other stuff that's happening to me is too humiliating to share. The doctors tell me if I agree to their treatment, I may have six months to a year ... and if I don't agree to their treatment, I may have six months to a year.' I held the silence and let her continue. 'You once told me we are not victims of our hereditary and that we are masters of our genetics. I had no idea what that meant at the time and I probably still don't, but I am willing to listen now.'

'What can I do to help, Sarah?' I needed to hear my friend say it first. The first step of healing is allowance. Allowance has a lot to do with how we heal and how we grow.

'I need more options, Pauline. You've told me stories of how you've healed yourself and helped others to heal themselves too. I need more options. Please give me more options.' Her voice trembled as tears of desperation fell from her cloudy blue eyes. 'I need to be in your orbit Pauline. I want to stick around. I don't want to die. Who will care for my kids? Tell me what to do. Please, tell me what to do.'

Sarah's depression, I had always known about. The lupus, I did not. The other condition, she finally admitted, was Crohn's disease. Of course I agreed to help my friend.

Jump forward again and the good news is that this conversation occurred two years ago. And a lot has happened for Sarah in the last two years.

When Sarah joined me on my living room sofa with our glasses of pinot noir, silence settled over us. My friend then shared with me two pieces of news. The first filled my heart with joy. The second made my pulse beat faster. She told me that her test results that morning revealed that she was finally in remission from the autoimmune condition that almost took her life two years ago. The medical team never expected her to be well again and at the very least not without major surgery.

She then told me that she had finally walked out of her buyer's agency business, shocking a lot of people along the way. We held one another for the longest time. Two friends in warm embrace, sobbing in each other's arms, filled with excitement and hope for a better tomorrow.

Ego says, 'Once everything falls into place, I will feel peace.'
Spirit says, 'Find your peace, and everything will fall into place.'
—Marianne Williamson

OPEN MIND, OPEN HEART

Sarah's healing was not a miracle. Sarah's healing was the result of having an open mind and an open heart. Before her healing process could commence, I made her promise that she would keep an open mind and an open heart. I made her promise to love herself enough to be present at all times and to never give up on the work, however long it took. It would take both her mind and her heart to work coherently, as well as immense love for herself if she was to heal. She found it difficult at first because the profoundly disruptive strategies shattered the way she had always seen herself and shattered the scientific and medical paradigm that she had always known and believed. We refocused the entire way she saw the world, and this opened up for her a vast new horizon of human potential.

The strategies used are not miracles but ancient tools and wisdoms combined with modern technologies that can be applied to everyday life. They are the same strategies I used to heal myself when the doctors suspected the anomalous growth in my left eye to be a tumour. What started as an annoying itch in the corner of my eye (which I had attributed to the advent of spring) became a full-blown condition that saw me admitted to the emergency ward. Over time, my eye had swollen shut and the chronic pain felt like a hot iron needle was searing through my left eye, lodging itself permanently in my brain and neck. The only way the doctors could be sure what the growth was, was to perform a biopsy.

The 'tumour' had grown to the size of a cherry when they operated. After the operation, the doctors were baffled. The symptoms were evident. The excruciating pain and inflammation was real. The X-rays and CT scans showed abnormalities but the biopsy report showed no trace of cancer cells. They had no explanation. Instead they pumped me with antibiotics and steroids for the entire week that I was kept under observation. Upon discharge from the hospital, they told me to continue with the steroid prescription and to come back in a month for a second operation. I thought the surgery was bad; however, nothing could have prepared me for the horrific side effects that prolonged steroid use inflicted upon my mind, my body and my spirit.

After leaving the hospital, I immediately sought advice from my network of progressive and alternative thinkers. There was no way I was returning to the hospital to have them cut me open again with no answers. What the doctors were telling me made no sense. Like Sarah, I needed more options. It was at this point that my world cracked open. It was at this point that I discovered the self-healing potential of the human body. Because I had asked the questions, the Universe provided, and I was introduced to energy healers, energy medicine, acupuncturists, spiritual teachers and shamans who used ancient traditions to master our healing potential.

As well, I learned from progressively thinking modern-day doctors, scientists and neuroscientists, who showed me the hard evidence behind new scientific discoveries in genetics, molecular biology and epigenetics as well as neurocardiology that now confirms what the many ancient traditions have been saying throughout history – that our bodies can heal themselves when given the right conditions. The trajectory of my life completely changed after this.

Exactly one month later, I honoured the appointment that I had made with the eye surgeon. Per his instructions, I got a CT scan of my eye prior to the appointment. When I showed him the report, I told him that there was no need for another operation. He studied the CT scan and tried to make sense of it. From his point of view, a miracle had happened. He wrote down the names of my energy healer, my acupuncturist as well as my science and spirituality teachers. He took notes as I told him of how I fasted and received daily acupuncture for two whole weeks. I told him how my spiritual teachers helped me to change the old stories and belief systems so that I could upgrade my biology. I told him of how my shaman taught me breathing techniques that enhanced my autonomic nervous system and altered my biochemistry. I told him how I committed to a one-hour meditation every single day so that I can train my mind to be the master of my body rather than defaulting to how it was before – where my body was in control of mind. He gathered the report papers and concluded, 'I will be sure to show this to the board.' I never heard from him again.

Who are we but the stories we tell ourselves, about ourselves, and believe. —Scott Turow

In his book *Human by Design: From Evolution by Chance to Transformation by Choice*, Gregg Braden writes,

> *As a trained scientist … what I can say is that new scientific discoveries have identified a link between specific healing modalities known in the past and their ability to restore balance in our bodies. It's the fact of this relationship that invites an honest reassessment of the limiting story we've been told about our origin as a species and what we're capable of. When we consider the facts revealed by the science of today, spontaneous healings and miracles such as the one I experienced seem less rare and extraordinary and more like an ordinary part of everyday life.*

We are conditioned to believe that we are insignificant and powerless to the world. We have been programmed to think that we have no influence over our bodies. Nothing could be further from the truth. Your genetics are not necessarily your destiny. Your epigenetics plays an equal role. Nature and nurture play together. We are not victims of our hereditary. We are masters of our genetics. We all have the power to self-regulate our own biology. No other form of life can do this. We have options on how we go about healing our bodies. We can now choose and, once we have decided, we can learn to awaken this technology. Only 5 per cent of disease is caused by our DNA and genetic coding while 95 per cent is epigenetics – genetic expression – the result of our perceptions of our experiences.

This speaks to the concept of 'entanglement'. The experiences you have with your family, your job, your relationships, your community and your environment affect your energy. If your work colleagues are toxic and your business environment breeds stress and frustration, this energy enters your field and you take these energies home and unwittingly share them with your family. We are all entangled. Your health is not what is under your skin. There is nothing in the cell that causes the disease. It is the environment in which the diseased cell is living that is the cause.

One of the big limitations that humanity holds is the concept that healing has to take a long time. It does not. Healing can be almost instantaneous. When you take a drug, only 1 per cent of the information is transferred to the cells – 99 per cent is lost as heat or wasted energy. Energy signals, on the other hand, are 100 times more efficient and infinitely faster than chemical signals. This is correlated to the quantum field. Many healers around the world demonstrate this and yet a strong conditioning within humanity thinks healing has to take a long time. Because you think it does, then in fact it does. It is our belief that controls our behaviour and our genes. The mind is the sole governing agency of the body. We carry within us a knowledge that is deep and it is powerful and it is beautiful. We just need to discover it for ourselves again.

Braden writes,

> When we think of ourselves separate from our bodies, we approach the healing process feeling like powerless victims of an experience that we have no control over. Conversely, recent discoveries confirm that when we approach life 'knowing' that our bodies are designed to constantly repair, rejuvenate, and heal, this shift in perspective creates the chemistry in our cells that mirrors the belief.

Steve Cole PhD, Professor of Medicine at UCLA School of Medicine, puts it this way: 'To an extent that immunologists and psychologists rarely appreciate, we are architects of our experience. Your belief carries more power than your reality.'

Our thoughts can make us sick – and make us well

Human beings, because of the size of their neo-cortex, can turn on the stress response by thought alone. That means our thoughts can make us sick. So if our thoughts can make us sick, is it possible that our thoughts can make us well? The answer is absolutely yes. Chronic stress can alter the immune system and increase dis-ease and the spread of tumour cells to the lymph nodes. Stress changes the function of the immune system and benefits tumours or cancer. Cancer cells hijack the lymphatic system and use it to travel around the body. Indeed, chronic stress can be the difference between a non-invasive stage zero cancer and an advanced stage four cancer. We have the capacity to self-regulate and tap into our subconscious to heal ourselves to release the neuropeptides that have stored themselves in our organs. So the power and the cure are in your thoughts. When you live a charged life and are inspired to assertively explore your environment to a greater degree, you grow more new neurons than if you were more passive. An article published in *Scientific American* in June 2002 writes that, 'The person with a rapidly growing tumour has a strong tendency to conceal his inner feelings and is less able to reduce tensions by doing something about them. Measures to relieve the psychological tension may prolong the life of the patient'. Change your mind and you will change the chemistry of your body.

Allopathic medicines attempt to alleviate the symptoms of disease by attacking or affecting the natural defences of the body, whereas homeopathy embraces the body's natural response system by either encouraging the symptoms of healing or attacking the root cause of the illness. Through energy work, I have experienced dozens of people having their physical bodies realigned from pain to joy and celebration within moments. When your energy centres start moving toward a more perfect alignment, the different elemental aspects of self (the physical, emotional, astral and so on) the physical body is in perfect health.

Embracing this new story comes with reluctance and resistance because doing so keeps us locked in the old stories that make us feel trapped and make us feel like victims. The new stories no longer keep us small and at the mercy of 'Big Pharma'. Braden continues,

> *There is rock solid scientific evidence that is not allowed in the mainstream because it will change the stories that keep us living in fear and keep us controlled. Science and medicine has been hijacked by corporate and religion.*

We know how far people will go to preserve the old story. It is not something to 'believe' as we now know how much belief can actually limit us. Money, power, habit and ego stop this information from going mainstream.

Dr Joe Dispenza, author of *Becoming Supernatural: How Common People Are Doing the Uncommon*, puts it this way:

If you look at Quantum Physics, which is the physics of possibility, you have to look at the spiritual aspects of ourselves because you couldn't explain a miracle, you couldn't explain a biological process, you couldn't explain the healing of a cut without understanding the quantum model of reality ... that there are particles – which are matter, which is you and I and everything in this physical world; and then there is energy, and that energy has a consciousness, it has an awareness, and that energy has a field of information that we are an extension of, and have access to. We spend so much of our lives looking outside of ourselves instead of looking inside of ourselves. We are conditioned to look for particles and matter instead of energy and information.

UCLA psychiatrist Dan Siegel in his book *Mind* supports this, arguing that consciousness – directed by intention, working through energy fields – can produce radical changes in matter. 'Skull and skin are not limiting boundaries of energy and information.'

It took less than a month to heal myself. Sarah's healing took two years. Sometimes it takes a long time; sometimes it takes no time at all. Every person is different, as is the healing required, and it is important to avoid overstating our human power. The length of time it takes, and the ultimate results, is left to the mystery of the Divine. Perhaps there are more lessons that we are meant to learn as we go through the process of removing the blocks that release a lifetime of buried trauma. Perhaps it takes some people longer than others to come to terms with how much work they are willing to commit to healing their internal ecology as well as their external kingdom. Perhaps the Universe knows what to put you through to get you closer to what is meant for you.

Indian religious leader Osho puts it like this:

People say, 'I want health' – and you go on clinging to your disease, and you don't allow the disease to go. If the doctor prescribes the medicine, you throw away the medicine; you never follow any prescription. You never go for a morning walk, you never go swimming, you never go running on the beach, you never do any exercise. You go on eating obsessively, you go on destroying your health – and again and again you go on asking where to find health. But you don't change the mechanism that creates unhealth. Health is not something to be attained somewhere, it is not an object. Health is a totally different way of living. The way you are living creates disease, the way you are living creates misery. Now people want happiness – but just by wanting, you cannot get it. Wanting is not enough. You will have to see into the phenomenon of your misery, how you create it – how in the first place you became miserable, how do you go on becoming miserable every day – what is your technique?

WAKE UP FROM DIS-EASE AND BECOME STRESS FREE

Through the continuous work that Sarah and I did together, she was finally able to wake up. For most of her life, she had been living by the hormone of stress and it had made her sick. Stress is the achiever's word for fear. Sarah had been addicted to the emotion of stress and was living in fear and she didn't even know it. For a year, her health didn't change much but she was determined to continue to do the work. She never gave up. By the start of the second year, her emotional and mental state improved. And as she continued to do the work, she was able to stop living by the hormone of stress. She changed her belief system and vanquished the old paradigms that made her sick. Before being diagnosed with a potentially terminal disease, your career and material achievements may dominate your mind; afterwards, however, your family, your health, your friends and your spirituality become the priority. Receiving a tenuous change of life can be a profound experience. It can deeply change our outlook on life and alter our behaviour. Emotional initiators, promoters and compounders all lead to the development of disease. This represents the last-ditch feedback effort of the physical body to reawaken the mind to the hidden order of truth and love. Prolonged contemplation of death produces shifts in personal values and goals,

Dis-ease is a summary of what we eat, what we drink, what we think, how we breathe and, most importantly, what we do not eliminate. Sarah cleaned up her body when she cleaned up her diet. She learned to truly love and care for herself again. By creating the optimum conditions in her internal and external world, we shifted Sarah's belief from powerless victim to powerful co-creator. She began to intentionally contour her thoughts when she tended to the fragile, neglected garden that was her mind. Thick weeds had grown in deep recesses over the years that she had paid no attention to her mind. She created time to meditate twice a day and went into nature every morning before work. Joy, gratitude, compassion, inspiration and appreciation became her default emotions.

By uniting the mystical and the practical, she had become the master of her mind, her body and their spirit. Her net health became just as important as her net wealth. She won her power back. Sarah had opened the door to the Universe and she became one with it instead of being separate to it. She became powerful, energetic, alert and present. Sarah no longer needed the cocktail of anti-depression medication that the doctors prescribed her and, over time, the lupus disappeared. Health and vitality returned when she regained her inner strength and inherent wisdom. Author and clinician Dr Dean Ornish writes, 'I am not aware of any other factor in medicine that has a greater impact on our survival that the healing power of love'. The emotional balancing power of transcendent love, and especially love for herself, was the greatest healer of all.

Most people wait for crisis or trauma or loss before they look into the business of change. It is when people truly reach the end of their beliefs, or when they are facing crisis in their life, that they start to look within and ask the bigger questions. The well-researched placebo effect is scientific proof that we have the ability to heal ourselves. Our thoughts are powerful enough to bring things into existence. By choosing your thoughts, and by selecting which emotional currents you will release and which you will reinforce, you will determine not only the quality of your health and wellbeing, but also the effects that you will have upon others, and the nature of the experiences of your life. Different choices lead to a new destiny. This is quantum physics at its most fundamental.

The work that Sarah and I did together is the same work that I love to teach as part of my Awaken the Spiritual Entrepreneur program. This is the work that brings me the most joy. As we delve into these intangible aspects of wellness and wellbeing, it becomes clear that there is more to the human experience than we can see under a microscope. And while spirit is not something we are able to measure on an individual level, we are able to see its qualitative impact on health in other ways. Nurturing the heart, the mind, the body and the soul must be of the utmost importance for any entrepreneur. Without true health, there can be no true wealth.

We all have a choice. We can change in a state of pain and suffering or we can change in a state of joy, great health and inspiration. The sad reality is that most wait for a crisis to happen before they change.

From healed pain comes wisdom

Sarah outgrew her business partner spiritually and left her buyer's agency business, upsetting a lot of people in the process. The business that once defined her now made her miserable. Going to work every day and being around the cutthroat culture of her business and the industry became toxic to her emotional and mental health. The greatest cause of split ups in business and in life is when one partner outgrows the other. Author George Leonard once put it this way: 'When your tennis partner starts improving his or her game and you don't, the game eventually breaks up. The same applies to relationships.'

Sarah now wanted to master her external world and build on their new entrepreneurial idea. She wanted to learn more and move even faster to build her new online business. It had always been her dream to have her own fashion accessory line but her father had always said it was too 'girly' a career and forced her into the real estate business. But Sarah possessed a new hunger now, and a new vision of how she wanted her life to be. In no time at all, her fashion accessory business exploded and pre-orders for her exclusive handbags and shoes were up over 100 per cent month on month. She was the person doing the marketing and driving the growth and managing the business and, often, she worked into the night. But she found a new energy and work no longer felt like work for her. She also started an online educational program to teach stay at home mums how to build an online business for themselves.

Her husband doted on her even more and supported every stage of her new venture. Her children were grateful to have their mother back – healthy, energised and thriving. She was not the same person she used to be and their children joked that they liked 'Mum version 2.0' much better. The things she used to tolerate become intolerable – she realised that certain situations no longer deserved her time, energy and focus. Where she once remained quiet, she now spoke her truth. Where she once battled and argued, she now chose to remain silent. She began to understand the value of her voice. But as with every new chapter in life, her changes came with new challenges. The biggest challenge she met on her new path of mastery was posed by her society. In a world where conformity is valued, peer groups at every stage of life exert a levelling influence.

Former work colleagues told her she was crazy for leaving the solid business that she had spent years creating. They told her she was stupid for leaving a secure income for something uncertain and unknown. Extended family attempted to make her feel guilty for being so ambitious in this new 'fluffy' career. They reminded her time and time again to maintain 'work–life balance' and to stop putting work first.

The unbridled release of human energy can be frightening

A new inspiration greeted Sarah every morning when she woke, however. Spiritual productivity filled her days. She was no longer waiting on the life she wanted, she was creating it. Sarah discovered a profound new way of loving herself and couldn't wait to get out of bed each day to make changes, meet challenges and create improvements to her business and her life. Making an impact in a state of creation excited her every day and fuelled their reason for being. Each morning, Sarah decided how she wanted to think and feel, and then rearranged all the people and circumstances in her life to make it so. She would make no apology to anyone for being passionately in love with life and her existence in it. She wanted to soar higher and gave up everything that weighed her down. She wanted to soar higher so that she could breathe in the rare air of truth and nonconformity. Truth became her companion when she found new eagles to fly with.

WORK–LIFE BALANCE IS BULLSHIT

Over the years, I have observed many people relentlessly pursue this thing they call 'work–life balance'. For me, it is a phrase that conjures up an image of me balancing on a tight rope, with work on one side and life on the other, desperately trying not to fall or fail.

The term work–life balance assumes that work is a burden, a place where there is not enough joy and fulfilment. And it is only on other side, in the life department, where experience is juicy and fun. The term work–life balance assumes that it is only in the life department where the stuff that matters really happens.

In reality, there is no such thing. Why? Because it's unattainable. It's not real. Mother Nature herself is not interested in balance. There are no straight lines in nature. If there was balance in nature, she would be void of the beauty and the extremes that make her a wonder to behold. There is only one theme in nature and that is progressive change – expansion and creation.

Work and life are not separate. They never have been. Work is part of who we are and what we do. We spend more time working than we do any other activity in our life except sleeping. So to suggest that work is separate from life is ridiculous.

I have never heard anyone say that they need to work more in order to improve their work–life balance. Have you? This is dysfunctional thinking that ignores the most basic and most important truth – that work doesn't have to suck!

People who love what they do and are good at it don't complain about work–life balance because it doesn't make any sense to them. People who love what they do are not itching for the weekend or counting down the hours to quitting time. They operate with integrity, mindfulness and flow. They don't need this artificial sense of balance because work feels good and natural to them. People whose values are aligned at work, at home and at play experience harmony and integration.

In his book *A New Earth*, Ekhart Tolle states that,

> *People who are exceptionally good at what they do perform largely free of ego while they work. They may not know it but their work becomes a spiritual practice. They are one with what they do and are fully present to respond to the task at hand.*

What if, instead of work–life balance programs, we started investing in teaching people and teaching organisations how to put people in jobs and positions where they can do what they love? Positions where they can do the things that come naturally to them. Where they can do the things that make them feel good. After all, fish are not meant to climb trees.

What if we taught people the self-awareness and self-understanding and self-esteem and self-mastery skills to get clear on their dreams and goals? What if we taught people that it was their responsibility to find a job that was fulfilling? What if we taught people that they were accountable for their own happiness? You don't like your job? Try harder. Still don't like your job? Then leave. You hate your boss? Work it out or find somewhere else. You don't have enough skills? Then learn. Find something you love to do somewhere you love to do it.

The Spiritual Entrepreneur is accountable for their own happiness. While other people talk about their 'careers' as their progress at work, or in their occupation or profession, the Spiritual Entrepreneur defines their career as who they are, the actions they take and who they want to become. They are constantly working in and on their career. It is the burning desire that fires inside their belly to achieve what they set out to achieve. It is the burning desire that tells them to go out, kick some arse, get shit done and be better than before.

When we do the uncommon and the unknown, people pay attention. When we are fuelled by courage, resilience and grit, and the relentless pursuit of a worthy ideal; when we want something badly enough that we will go out and fight for it, to work day and night for it, to give up our time and sleep for it, to bleed, sweat and cry for it; and when we can do so without the guilt, then we can start talking about work–life harmony and integration, instead of work–life balance and separation.

Happiness happens when we fit with all aspects of our lives – our heart, our mind, our health and our spirit. Happiness happens when we are living our life's mission and we are fulfilled. When we fit so harmoniously that whatever we are doing is our joy.

GETTING CLEAR ON YOUR DREAMS AND GOALS

In the previous chapters, we discussed the importance of finding your mission and how to operate from purpose. We identified your truest and highest values and priorities and you become aware of your most heartfelt mission and inspiring vision. Now it's time to set goals and objectives that are congruent with your vision. This chapter offers tips surrounding goals and mapping out your path so that you can create a meaningful, purposeful and fulfilling life. Goals are great but if they are not fuelled by a strong purpose, it is like trying to drive a high-performance car without an engine. You need to have the engine and the fuel to drive it.

As you move toward deepening your success in absolutely every dimension of your life, it is important to have a clear goal, but it is not so important to have a clear map on how you'll achieve your goal. Yes, you'll need to take action, but it's not necessary to meticulously plot out every step. Think of your goal as the destination, and mapping as the route you will plot to get there.

Some goal-setting gurus encourage us to be extremely specific, and to map out every step of the journey to the goal. But that's like jumping into a taxi at Heathrow Airport and asking to go to Mayfair and then micromanaging every step of the journey from the back seat. London taxi drivers are highly trained. Attempting to give direction from the back seat would be unnecessary and almost insulting to the driver. And the Universe is a billion times more intelligent than a London taxi driver. (No offence to taxi drivers.)

Those who are starting out on their goal setting and manifestation journey think that they have to be incredibly specific about the details to the Universe. Indeed specificity is powerful. Yes, you have to be specific with what you want – the destination – but when you start to get a little more advanced and have a little more in your spiritual bank account, you will realise that the Universe always has something even better for you in mind. It's like going to a fancy restaurant and having no desire to look at the menu. Instead you let the chef send out an exquisite ten-course degustation menu with matching wines and it is all delicious and divine. You could never have ordered those dishes in that sequence with that artistry. The chef knows so much more about the intricacies of this cuisine than you ever will. This is where we ultimately want to get with our goal setting – yes, we have to start placing our order, but eventually we have to trust that the chef knows better than we do.

When you have a goal and place the intention, the very act of you striving to become more and reaching deep inside of you to find the creative essence is the catalyst.

The very thought of your goal and desire signals your biology to find the space in the quantum field. The quantum field is the field of information and infinite possibilities and potential, based on the fact that we can design a future based on the way we think and act. The Universe knows the destination you want before you even say it. It's like a telepathic Siri. What's more impressive is that it planted in you the idea to request the specific destination you have chosen. That's right – the Universe gave you the idea to request your current destination. If it didn't plant it, then you wouldn't have the idea.

There is one caveat, however. You must act quickly! In the quantum model of reality, the faster you get the inspiration and take action, the more inspiration you're going to get. If you hesitate and don't act quickly, the energy that the quantum field gifted to you in the way of inspiration will lose its charge. The idea will tire of waiting for you and the 'ideas fairies' will give the opportunity to someone else if you don't get your idea out into the world first. We hear it all the time – someone across the world, 'Stole my idea!' No, they didn't. Your thought, your idea, your goal, popped up in the quantum field as a potential as soon as you thought about it. You just didn't act on it fast enough.

So, if you are not in a position to take massive action toward your goal, you must begin to at least take small steps in the direction that you think may inspire you. Take the first step. Move into the direction of your soul's nudging and you will gain the support of nature. If you know what you need to do – if you know your purpose, life gets very easy. Whether small steps or massive steps, you wake up and just do it. And as you take another step, life reveals itself to you a little more. Most people get frustrated and stressed worrying about what they're supposed to do; they don't know what they're supposed to do because they don't know what they want. And if you don't know what you want, you don't know what to do.

So decide what you want, and once you have decided, it is the Universe's pleasure to fulfil your goals and aspirations, because it is the Universe who authored them. So we have to get comfortable being in the unknown. One of life's greatest joys is that our freedom is determined by the degree to which we can rest in the unknown. When you comprehend that your life was created by and belongs to the Universe, and that your life is an expression of something much bigger than your mere individuality, you will understand that anything is possible.

Mastering your internal and external kingdom

There is another caveat, however, as you set out towards your goal, and that is you must feel inspired and happy heading in the direction chosen. If you don't feel happy and inspired, you may personally be resisting a needed change and be personally holding on to something you have outgrown. Herein lies our biggest challenge as creators. The lack we live by each day when we notice our goal hasn't happened yet causes us to feel separate from our dreams, and we no longer believe in our future. That is because we are back in the emotions of our past – and we can't see our future through the window of our past. When we live in lack while we are still creating our future, over time we stop creating and wait for something outside of us to take away the lack we feel inside of us. But it is the lack that is keeping our dreams at arm's length in the first place.

Quantum physics is the physics of feeling. We create what we feel. What we feel we create. Whatever your dream and your goal is, ask yourself: How does it feel? How does it feel when you are visioning your dreams? How does it feel when you experience love, joy, gratitude, freedom and abundance? If you align yourself to that frequency level, you will experience that potential. What if you lived by the emotions of your future every day? You would feel like your future has already happened and would be less likely to feel separate from your dreams. That's how we believe in a future we have not yet experienced with our senses, yet we keep it alive in our mind and body. If we keep thinking about making that future become a reality, we naturally begin to insert ourselves into the scene of our future.

According to research on mental rehearsal, once we immerse ourselves in that scene, changes begin to take place in our brain. Therefore, each time we do this, we are laying down new neurological pathways in the present moment that literally change our brain to look like the brain of our future. In other words, the brain starts to think like the future we want to create has already happened. So, the important big picture question you need to ask yourself whenever you have a goal or a dream is this: how do I align my vibration and my frequency to match the potential that already exists in the quantum field right now?

What do I need to do to feel the way I want to feel? Feed your soul and your passion. Do whatever it is that makes you feel like you're living your life to the fullest. Hold onto that frequency and watch the world around you shift in astounding ways.

Like an individual wave that is connected to an almighty ocean, you have the power of the vast ocean behind you at all times. The wave on its own is miniscule. But with the ocean behind it, it is all-encompassing and completely powerful. Remember – it is important to be clear about the destination and to take action but leave the specific details on how to get there to nature. The important thing to remember about goal setting is that you don't need to control. The Universe's GPS is supreme; it knows the most circuitous route – and circuitous route because the most direct route may not be the right route. Lessons can be learned, big and small on a longer journey. There are new people to meet, new voices to be heard, new concepts to learn and new experiences to be had – all of which prepare us for the final destination of this particular vision.

If we get tunnel vision, and attempt to micromanage every step on our route, we could miss the fact that we are sitting next to a woman on the plane who has the power through one flick of her pen to create a massive leap in our business and our life.

THREE SPIRITUAL SECRETS FOR GOAL SETTING

When setting your dreams and goals, you need to be aware of three spiritual secrets. These are:

1. *The means has to equal the ends.* When we have a goal that we are heading towards, the 'means' (the action we take now) must equal the 'ends' (the result we'd like to create in the future).

   The destination we are seeking should translate to the experience of fulfilment, peace, freedom, good relationships, abundance and so on; however, one can't expect to arrive at a destination of balance and happiness in the future through being unbalanced and unhappy in the now. If we reset in the state of gratitude and give thanks to a new life before it is made manifest, we are ahead of our time because gratitude is the ultimate state of receivership. To rest in a state of gratitude means that the event has already happened.

2. *You don't know what's up ahead from where you're standing now.* When we set goals we do so in real time, meaning we create goals in the now in the absence of data to do with events and situations in the future. From a spiritual point of view, we don't want to be rigidly attached to achieving a goal because it presents as a particular form.

   Sarah had a goal to be a successful buyer's agent, but when she created that goal she did so in the absence of the knowledge that she would not enjoy the day-to-day of the job. We don't want to feel wedded to a trajectory for our life that was created historically. Who you are today could be different and more evolved than the person you were when you set that goal. If you're making yourself consistently miserable trying to achieve a goal, change the goal.

3. *All roads lead back to you and the now.* Preachers, prophets and sages, from time immemorial, have all taught that the happiness we seek resides inside us, and is accessible now. For the most part, our culture teaches the opposite – that happiness and fulfilment live on the yonder side of future achievement. The minds says, 'Once I acquire a certain "experience" in the future, I will be happy and fulfilled.' Interestingly, when we analyse the acquisition of any goal, what we are actually aspiring toward is an experience. When we buy possessions such as houses, cars or boats, what we are buying is the experience that we hope the particular object will provide. What we acquire in terms of material possessions translates and culminates as an experience.

   How will you feel when you live in this house? How will you feel when you drive that car? It is wise to remember that when we experience anything, we experience that thing in the now.

We can't experience the future, now.

We can't experience the past, now.

We can only experience the now, now.

Now is the only thing we truly have and it is the gateway to all experience. Therefore, now is more precious than gold. It is more valuable than your most prized possession because it is the portal through which we experience all of our possessions. Now is the gateway through which we experience our greatest adventures and our greatest loves; it is the gateway through which we experience our life. So we need to be mindful that we don't sacrifice, undersell, or gamble away now. Many sacrifice the now in the hope of acquiring a better experience in the future. 'I will postpone doing things I love now, because I will feel better then.' But sometimes 'then' doesn't come. And when 'then' comes, it arrives as now.

In the pursuit of our goals, it is wise to remember that to increase the quality of our experience of the future, we need to increase the quality of our experience in the now.

So if we have aspirations to 'eventually' be happy and 'eventually' live our lives with joy later, we need to be happy now. If we are happy now, we will be happy later. Enjoy the journey now because now is all we have. Now is the only thing that is real.

> *We shall not cease from exploration, and the end of all our exploring will be to arrive where we started and know the place for the first time.* —TS Eliot

Set goals and contemplate them daily

You also need to set goals and contemplate them daily, for three reasons:

1. *Doing so gives direction to your life.* Can you imagine boarding an ocean liner where the captain doesn't know the destination? Ridiculous, right? It would never happen. Living life without goals is like a ship's captain not knowing the next port of call.

2. *We tend to create that which we can imagine.* If you can't imagine climbing Mount Everest, you won't even attempt the summit. Everything that was created by humans in the world in front of our eyes was once an idea in the world behind our eyes in the realm of thought.

3. *Having clear goals gives us something inspiring and exciting to move towards.* Even if we don't achieve the goal, we would find the quality of our experience in the now enhanced because our life is oriented in a positive creative direction.

THE RISKS OF NOT HAVING GOALS

If we don't have goals, we risk three things:

1. We run the risk of aimlessly drifting around, majoring in minors — meaning we can get lost in the activity of being busy for the sake of being busy.

2. We get swept up in someone else's vision, because the people with the biggest and most compelling visions tend to excel in business and thus create the means to employ others. Nothing is wrong with working for others; however, if you are an entrepreneur, chances are you will prefer to capture your own vision and devote your time and energy to its creation. Having goals helps with that. The greater your goals, the greater your life.

3. Without goals, we can rob ourselves of the possibility of unlocking our full potential and thus we can die not even knowing the full extent of our capabilities.

What to remember when setting goals

And finally, you need to know three specific aspects when setting goals:

1. It is important to set goals that you can describe in a few short sentences, because if you are writing epic-length goals, you are simply not going to find the time to sit down and re-read them.

2. Capture both the feel and visual image of each of your goals using one sentence. That way, you can contemplate them for sixty seconds and be done.

3. Goals should be written in orbit around your personal priorities and principles. They should also be written in the present tense.

Having a few short goals that you can read daily is the key to getting in and staying within Quadrant 4.

Two famous quotes hang on my office wall. Both serve to remind me that nature wants to support me in all my endeavours and that the Universe has my back, cheering me on all the way. Perhaps you would like to place these quotes on your wall too.

> *Until one is committed, there is hesitancy, the chance to draw back, always ineffectiveness. Concerning all acts of initiative and creation, there is one elementary truth the ignorance of which kills countless ideas and splendid plans: that the moment one definitely commits oneself, then providence moves too. All sorts of things occur to help one that would never otherwise have occurred. A whole stream of events issues from the decision, raising in one's favour all manner of unforeseen incidents and meetings and material assistance, which no man could have dreamed would have come his way. Whatever you can do or dream you can do, begin it. Boldness has genius, power, and magic in it. Begin it now.* —Johann Wolfgang von Goethe

> *And, when you want something, all the universe conspires in helping you to achieve it.* —Paolo Coehlo, *The Alchemist*

Remember – without our health, there can be no wealth. The Spiritual Entrepreneur is not interested in instant gratification; they are in this game long term. It is longevity in business and in life that is important to them. The Spiritual Entrepreneur understands that creating an extraordinary quality of life requires a paradigm shift from managing their time to managing their energy, managing their thoughts, and managing their life. They understand the importance of achieving the goals that they set for themselves, and that their goals must encompass all areas of their life, including their mind, their heart, their health and their spirit. The Spiritual Entrepreneur is not so focused on their businesses that they neglect their health. Self-sustainability is key. They understand that they are not a victim of their hereditary – they are the master of their genetics. What they feed their body is just as important as what they feed their mind and their spirit.

The Spiritual Entrepreneur understands that they are not a powerless victim. They are a powerful co-creator of their life. It is only when they dare to stand at the mirror naked and ruthlessly interrogate themselves that they can truly see themselves and truly know themselves. When we do not know who we really are is when we grasp onto the confusion. When we truly know ourselves, we can begin to truly heal ourselves. To truly heal ourselves is to truly love ourselves. When love and truth and skill and wisdom work together, a masterpiece comes to life. The Spiritual Entrepreneur understands that the only impossible journey is the one they never begin, and that the secret to living an extraordinary life is not the pursuit of happiness, but happiness in the pursuit.

'The Way' Secret #6

INNER PEACE, OUTER ABUNDANCE

When I run after what I think I want, my days are a furnace of stress and anxiety; if I sit in my own place of patience, what I need flows to me, and without pain.

From this I understand that what I want also wants me, is looking for me and attracting me. There is a great secret here for anyone who can grasp it.

—Rumi

THE BUSINESS OF HEARTS

When the moon peeped over the glittering city skyline, our guests began spilling through our restaurant doors. They were here to help us celebrate Red Lantern's 16th birthday. As always, what followed was a heartfelt evening full of joy, love, deep gratitude and surprise – the four most powerful emotions that connect human beings together. The heart of our restaurant beat in unison with the hearts of our most loyal guests and raving fans.

Having lasted for sixteen years places Red Lantern in the top 4 per cent of businesses in the world – those that have survived more than ten years in business. Two questions I am often asked in business inter-views and entrepreneurial conversations go something like this: 'How is it that Red Lantern is still around after so many years? And what do you do to compete in such a tumultuous, fickle, competitive, satu-rated and challenging industry?' My answer always throws them. You see, we don't view the top restaurants in Sydney as our competitors. We are our biggest competitors. We must run our own race. Why would we waste our valuable time and our valuable energy worrying about what the others are doing? We prefer to focus our valuable time and our valuable energy on what matters most. It is our own internal ecology that matters most. Much can be said for still staying in the game long after the others have given up. The Universe rewards the unreasonably determined.

That night, the emotional speeches brought a tear to many, and the auspicious lion dance marked the auspicious occasion. Red Lantern's award-winning food and matching wines were perfectly seasoned with the laughter, conversations and good cheer that filled the room. The friendships and connections we have built over the years have made our hearts sing. My brother Luke flew in especially to join us and my husband, Mark, was on form. The most beautiful moment of the night was when Mark recognised each member of the Red Lantern team with real love and affection. Each staff member was given their own special moment to shine after years of dedicated service and hard work.

On average, our team members stay working with us for six to ten years. Our restaurant sees a miniscule staff turnover rate of 10 per cent, which is otherwise unheard of in the hospitality industry. Staff engagement and staff retention is a key item that entrepreneurs and corporations alike ask me to speak about on stage. Of course, we have had our fair share of employees who have not worked out, and we are not immune to the odd recruitment disaster either. It is the nature of any business. Luckily for us, these are a tiny percentage.

I have watched leadership speakers present many leadership tips, tricks and teachings on stage. I have heard them all and have, at some stage or another, implemented them. Some work. Most don't. Another question I am often asked in business interviews and entrepreneurial conversations goes something like this: 'How is it that Red Lantern is so successful in having your staff love where they work and buy in to the Red Lantern values so completely?' The secret here lies beyond personality profiling, 360-degree feedback tools, monthly appraisals and team-building exercises. The secret lies within our credo: 'To uplift the human spirit through the alchemy of flavour, hospitality and heart.' We are in the business of not only food, wine and service, but also touching hearts and sharing what it means to be human. Indeed, while Red Lantern's quality produce and world-class service is what we are famous for, it is within the understanding of the human spirit and the human heart that we can become masters of influence in our businesses and our lives. It is our human hearts that are the most powerful asset of our business.

> *To be successful you have to have your heart in your business and your business in your heart.* —Thomas J Watson Jr

In school we were taught that the main purpose of the heart was to pump blood through the body. Ancient traditions, however, have always held that the heart is the centre of deep wisdom, emotion and memory, as well as serving as a portal to other realms of existence. New scientific evidence now shows that the heart is the master organ of the body – that is, it is the heart that runs the show and not the brain (which is the common misconception). We now know that we have three intelligent and central brains: our mind, which is our cognitive aspect that processes our thoughts and gives us inspiration; our gut, which is our instinctive aspect that provides our 'gut instincts' and nourishes us; and our heart, which processes our emotions and allows us to access intuition and gives us joy.

Scientific discoveries led by J Andrew Armour, MD, PhD, of the University of Montreal, show us that our hearts are capable of something much more mysterious, powerful and beautiful than simply being a pump. The new science has proven what ancient wisdom has known all along – that the little brain in the heart can also think and feel and remember. In Amour's words, 'It has become clear in recent years that a sophisticated two-way communication occurs between the heart and the brain, with each influencing the other's function.' These discoveries have the potential to forever change the way we think of ourselves. They give new meaning to what is possible in our bodies and what we are capable of achieving in our lives.

THE HEART-BRAIN CONNECTION

What does this all mean for the Spiritual Entrepreneur and their businesses? It gives us the unquestionable competitive edge in business and in life.

Let's break it down.

Your brain

The brain, according to neuroscience, is organised to reflect our own personal environment and our own personal life – the people, the circumstances and the conditions in which we live are organised in the neurological structures in our brains. Your brain is setting you up to match your beliefs with what you think. When we give the neuron the right signal, it looks for other neurons to hook up with and harmonise with. Your brain will create the chemistry to match the picture in your mind – it decides what chemistry goes into the blood and how we see the world. So our belief indeed becomes more powerful than our reality.

Your thoughts

Interestingly, according to cognitive neuroscientists, only 5 per cent of our thoughts are conscious and determined by our prefrontal cortex, which speaks to our identity, source and spirit – the parts that are moving toward wishing and desire, aspiration and creation. So most of our decisions, actions, emotions and behaviour depend on the 95 per cent of brain activity that goes beyond our conscious awareness – including the subconscious thoughts that are based on habitual instincts and old programming. And of those subconscious thoughts, 75 per cent are negative and limited thoughts based on acquired behaviour and belief.

Your heart

The heart's brain is a network of neurons and neurotransmitters and proteins and supported cells similar to those found in the cranial brain. The heart's brain allows it to act independently of the cranial brain. The brain receives signals from the heart and the neuropeptides in our body create the chemistry to relive the experience and create the emotion that determines the perceptions we have in life. Every trauma that we have creates a hormone that mirrors that emotion. We all have different levels of trauma in our bodies and we are usually so scared to feel the pain that we continue to repress it and live under the illusion that the trauma is who we are. If you have unresolved trauma and you don't know how to deal with the emotion, it becomes disease. This can also happen with joy, but we don't get stuck on joy.

The heart and brain can work together in a state of harmony and flow

Your heart is 100,000 times stronger electrically and up to 5000 times stronger magnetically than the brain. Your heart is also 100 times greater in amplitude than the electrics of the brain. The heart-brain is intrinsic to your energy flow and intuition, and your ability to be in tune with the right decisions. When we have heart–brain coherence, it means that our heart (feelings and spirit) is in rhythmic flow and harmony with our mind brain (thoughts and cognition). Coherence is the heart and brain operating synergistically, like two systems that mesh into one. The practice of sitting in heart–brain coherence accumulates higher vibrational energy that has a carryover effect through our day. When we do this, our creative solutions for personal, social and global challenges become more accessible, providing us with more intuitive access and flow.

When people hold genuine core heart feelings such as appreciation, compassion, gratitude and care, it naturally increases their heart–brain coherence. Studies show that achieving heart–brain coherence opens the doorway to the subconscious mind and taps into a treasure chest of riches which include:

- accessing the greatest creative flow imaginable

- becoming cognitively smarter – including having more clarity and efficacy of thought

- achieving career brilliance – becoming more visionary and smarter, with higher level intelligence

- obtaining a supercharged ability to think creatively and dialogue effectively

- increased ability to make dynamic decisions

- increased states of consciousness, mindfulness and awareness

- increased power to connect and influence others in a positive way

- creating a direct heart communication with sensory neurites in other organs in the body

- gaining the heart-based wisdom known as heart intelligence

- increased desire for collaboration

- increased intuitive problem-solving and decision-making

- achieving intentional states of deep intuition

- gaining intentional precognitive abilities

- awakening super-learning abilities

- gaining the power to manifest more of what you want in life
- increasing your mechanisms of intentional self-healing
- releasing old wounds and trauma
- increased courage, resilience and grit
- increased energy levels
- enhanced states of joy and love
- enhanced states of inner child playfulness
- gaining 'off the charts' states of bliss
- achieving a deeper connection to your life passion and purpose

... and much, much more!

HOW HEART ENTRAINMENT INFLUENCES EVERYONE AROUND US

Heart 'entrainment' occurs when you connect with someone on a feeling and emotional level that is beyond the usual mental intellect. It is when both hearts beat in sync to the same pulse and rhythm and a synergy occurs as they fall into a similar vibrational pattern. The HeartMath Institute, based in California, provides the science to prove the power of heart–brain coherence and heart entrainment. Their research suggests that our energetic or spiritual heart is an access point for our natural inner technology – our heart's intuitive intelligence – which can elevate our communications, decisions and choices to a much higher level of effectiveness.

The following figure shows the Torus Field – the electromagnetic energy field that comes from the heart.

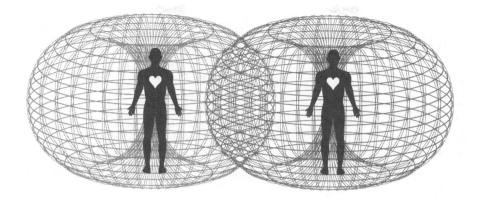

The research from the HeartMath Institute (www.heartmath.org) explores the interaction that takes place between one person's heart and another's brain when two people touch or are in proximity. Their findings show that the electromagnetic signals generated by the heart have the capacity to affect others around us through social coherence. The data indicates that one person's heart signal can affect another's brainwave and that heart–brain synchronisation can occur between two people when they interact.

Every human being radiates a double-torus electromagnetic energy field that is measurable several feet away. Our thoughts and emotions affect the heart's magnetic field, which in turn energetically affects those in our environment whether we are conscious of it or not. When we are experiencing elevated emotions such as love, joy, inspiration, compassion and freedom, the size of this energy field expands to encompass a greater amount of space – we are in high vibration. When we are depressed, feeling defeated, or otherwise dis-eased, this energy field shrinks much closer to the body – we are in low vibration.

When we are in close proximity to others, the frequency of our own field is in constant interaction with the other fields in a dynamic relationship. Your field is constantly interacting and enjoining with the fields of others. This interaction has a direct subconscious influence on you each and every time, regardless of whether or not your personal beliefs allow for the conscious acceptance of non-physically acquired information.

One thing I know to be true, having served over a million people in the 16 years that Red Lantern has been in business, is that the heart never lies. The intuition of our customers can sniff out the authentic passion in what we do. If you speak from the heart, do business from the heart, market your message from the heart, serve your customers from the heart, tell your story from the heart and live your life with an open heart, your spirit soars and you entrain others to do the same. This is how sustainable relationships are formed. An open heart has the power to ignite many. When you can uplift the human spirit with your open heart, you will find that you do not need to 'hard sell' your goods and services. You heart does much of the work, and on a much deeper energetic level. When you can uplift the human spirit, your staff will stay with you for many years and your customers will keep coming back to you because you make them feel good.

This equates to a more joyful and profitable experience in your business and your life.

GAINING GREATER POWER THROUGH HEART–BRAIN COHERENCE

Most of us know what it feels like when we are we are in a state of harmony and flow, when our hearts and minds are working together and we feel a genuine connection with others involved. Heart–brain coherence is not an idle state; it reaches out and influences and supports others in a plethora of beneficial ways. It's easy to love this experience of synergy. But oftentimes this happens by chance, rather than by design or intention. Wouldn't it be wonderfully advantageous to be able to produce this state of flow on demand in our day-to-day communications in business and in life?

In my advanced programs, I have designed my own unique technique to achieve heart–brain coherence by combining qigong breathing and a meditation curriculum. Specific breathing techniques can immediately change our biochemistry and help to harmonise the body and spirit by filling the organs and meridians with fresh qi energy. The breathwork that I teach increases oxygen levels to the blood, reducing stress and promoting deep states of bliss. My techniques are intentionally simple and effective.

As we learn to slow down our mind and attune to our deeper heart feelings, a natural intuitive connection can occur. Intuition is the Spiritual Entrepreneur's greatest superpower. Intuitive insights often unfold more understanding of ourselves, others, issues and life than years of accumulated knowledge. Your higher mind intuition is your ability to acquire and demonstrate knowledge without interference or the act of using reasoning from a position of factual knowing or evidence assumed to be true. Your intuition is a kind of inner perception that reveals that which is being ignored in your immediate and generally outer awareness. It can allow you to make relatively fast decisions without having to compare options. Your intuition helps lead you to inspired thoughts.

Now, imagine the magic that can happen when an entire organisation has heart–brain coherence and entrainment! The group are not only in sync, but are connected and communicating on an unseen energetic level. This kind of coherent group cooperation results in increased flow and strengthened relationships.

Connection is why we are here. Connection is what gives our lives meaning and purpose.

> *If man can control his mind he can find the way to Enlightenment, and all wisdom, virtue and any desire will naturally come to him.* —Buddha

Personal mastery must come first

It is clear that the practice of heart–brain coherence and entrainment supercharges our power of influence, not only at the energy vibration level at which the heart operates, but also on a biophysical communication level. One thing I know, having been involved in the entrepreneurial world since the age of seven, is that the game of business mastery is the game of mastering influence. And the first person we must have major influence over is ourselves. Personal mastery is key.

It has been my observation that most Entrepreneurs don't have business problems; they have personal problems that reflect in their business. As the leader, we must continuously do the inner work to fortify our inner core. As the leader, we are not only responsible, but also response-able. In the face of any adversity (and there are many in the life of an entrepreneur) it is our responsibility to remain cool and calm under pressure – to not freak out or play victim or complain about our perceived problems. Spirituality, therefore, is dealing with and handling all situations from a higher perspective.

As the leader, it is our responsibility to extract as much positive value and make as many empowering meanings from any challenge that comes our way. We must constantly rewire our emotional architecture. It is our internal ecology that matters most – we must keep strong the gatekeepers of our mind and our heart, for it is our internal ecology that will directly project and directly reflect on our external kingdom. We attract what we think and how we feel.

Entrepreneurs clearly face many challenges on our tumultuous journey. Much is at stake. The pressure is immense. Our balls are always on the line, so to speak. Let's face it: it is difficult to remain calm when you don't know whether or not you can make payroll. It is difficult to find composure when an unexpected tax bill arrives and clears out the cash in your bank account. It is difficult to feel confident when the economic downturn sees no customers come through your doors. It is difficult to wake up energised in the morning when you have no cash flow to speak of to pay the debt collectors and suppliers. It is difficult to stay cool when you don't know if you can generate enough income to pay your children's school fees. It is difficult to stay upbeat and cheerful when your spouse is depressed and suicidal. But these are the most important times to dig deep and show up with dignity, grace and poise. No. Matter. What.

Your people will not stick by a leader who is constantly stressed, fearful, angry, confused, mean spirited and bitter. Your people will follow the one who incites the most hope. The one who is the most composed and confident. The one who is charged with the energy of inspiration on a daily basis. The one who believes in something bigger than themselves. The one who shows unwavering internal certainty. The one who masters their energy and trains their mind to stay calm in any situation. To be calm in turmoil becomes a revolutionary act. As the leader, we are always being watched.

We must lead by example. What makes a Spiritual Entrepreneur an exceptional leader is not only emotional mastery but also energy mastery. When we are calm and in control, our intelligence and problem-solving skills cannot be robbed from us by the disempowering emotions that overtake and control us. This is a practice that needs to be cultivated. We must learn to stop disempowering emotion before it affects our neurocircuitry. When we are in a state of stress and panic, we only use 10 per cent of our mental, emotional and physical capabilities. By mastering more of ourselves, we have access to more of the other 90 per cent. We must refuse to allow stress, limited states and toxic people to rob us of our intelligence. We must examine and evolve not only our food consumption but also our news and media consumption, any useless and random information that we digest on social media, as well as violent and depressing movies or stories. Remember, rubbish in, rubbish out. Clean up your external influences so that you acquire additional energy rather than have your energy stolen from you. After all, the quality of our emotions is the game of life.

One thing I have learned through direct experience, as well as coaching and mentoring many established entrepreneurs over the years, is that the health of the business is a reflection of the health of the owner. Our level of consciousness has a profound effect on our businesses. Every thought, every action, creates ripples through this infinite field of consciousness. We are far more powerful than we realise. It is when our businesses falter that we have the opportunity to look within and ask the important questions. Where and when have I fallen unconscious as the leader? Am I currently living by the hormone of stress and anxiety? Is this why my staff are quitting? When and where did I fall from grace? Is my constant complaining depreciating my electromagnetic signature into the field? Is this why customers are repelled from doing business with me? Is my fear of losing everything attracting more fear and more loss? Are my internal uncertainty and deterioration the cause of the uncertainty and deterioration in my business?

CALM COURAGE IS CONTAGIOUS; SO IS FEAR

The new science of epigenetics states that we are not prewritten beings. Consciousness itself, our interpretation of an event, and the meaning we place on the event, can have a real effect at our genetic level and the way our genetic software expresses itself. Even the way we frame the story and the choice of words and language structure we use to mould the experience can change the physical expression of our cellular biology.

Epigenetics says that our perception is filtered through our internal processing system, which determines our state, physiology, behaviour and environment. So the cells that compose our body are actually the technology that turns experience into biology. And the ripple effects can impact five levels deep, affecting our team members, our customers, our friends, our spouses, our children, our children's school friends and so on.

How we perceive things and how we feel is at the very core of whether we manifest a desired outcome or an undesired outcome in our business and our lives. Our environment becomes us and we become our environment. We must choose them well. The good news is that, once we realise that we are somehow responsible for the outcome, we can step up, snatch our power back and overturn the situation.

Once we realise that we are constantly composing our own gene expression and its biological unfolding, we can take control of ourselves, our lives and our businesses again. When we truly want something and go after it without limiting ourselves with disbelief, the Universe will make it happen. So, if the new science says that good thoughts create good events and great thoughts create great events and that we can design before we can become, then we might as well get really good at it!

INCREASING YOUR DESERVING POWER

Your beliefs become your thoughts, your thoughts become your words, your words become your actions, your actions become your habits, your habits become your values, your values become your destiny. —Commonly attributed to Mahatma Gandhi

So how do we get really good at designing great events? How do we remain cool, calm and composed when things get tough? How can we manifest a favourable outcome in the face of any adversity? If we can understand that the main lesson we are put on this earth to learn is to relate to emotions and limitations, we can understand that obtaining personal mastery over our emotions and limitations is the key to increasing our deserving power in business and in life. If we desire to create an abundance of anything externally, we need to feel abundant internally. It is difficult to attract riches if we feel poor. And if we have all the riches and still feel poor, what is the point in that?

Many are under the illusion that it works in reverse. Give me the money and I'll feel rich. Or give me the relationship and then I'll feel love. But the Spiritual Entrepreneur knows that everything streams forth from the inside out. Feel rich and you will attract the money. Feel the love and you will attract the relationship. The thought sends the signal out into the quantum field and the feeling draws the event back to you. The world in front of our eyes is a visible and physical expression of an invisible mental and spiritual counterpart. If you want to change what you are creating externally, you need to change what you are thinking and feeling internally. We have to fully become the person we wish to attract before we see the manifestation of this in person. As entrepreneur and author Jim Rohn said, 'Success is not to be pursued; it is to be attracted by the person you become.'

We all have an inner sense of what we feel we deserve, and our deserving power to a large extent dictates the quality of our experiences. We cannot create more of anything we desire in our life, whether more money, more recognition or even love, unless we feel we deserve it. It doesn't matter what the current circumstances of your life are, you cannot feel that you deserve more if you are living in fear and in lack.

Your current financial status is unimportant if you want access into the higher levels of happiness and wealth.

If you want to tap into the abundance that Quadrant 4 success provides, you must live by elevated emotions in order to feel that you deserve it. You must cultivate the pure energy of creation to match your dream, and emulate this creation field by being as much like it as possible. Co-creation is cooperatively using the energy from the quantum field – the invisible field of Spirit. It is in the contemplation of this power that you actually acquire this power. This involves your willingness to contemplate yourself as being the magnet that attracts the conditions you desire to produce.

No matter how difficult the circumstances, you must make room mentally and in your heart for elevated emotions such as joy, peace, compassion, inspiration, freedom and love. No matter how difficult the circumstances, you must stay focused on the outcome that you really want and keep strong the gatekeepers of your mind and your heart. You cannot manifest wealth and abundance by continuously worrying about the impossibility of that happening. Be your own gatekeeper. Do not let anything or anyone in who is not willing to meet your divine desires. People talk about tolerance being a virtue – I say intolerance is also a virtue. If you want to fly, give up everything that weighs you down. To be yourself in a world that is constantly trying to make you something else is the greatest accomplishment.

Don't let the naysayers, the dream stealers and the sleepwalkers sway you from this extremely important task of co-creating your life. When you know where you want to go, you know what to take with you. More importantly, you will know who you need in your orbit to get you to your destination faster. Surround yourself with people who fuel optimism instead of pessimism. Surround yourself with people who believe in you. Surround yourself with people who believe in themselves. Choose your circle wisely.

The quality of your thinking will determine the quality of your business and your life. Don't make excuses for why you can't get it done. Focus on all the reasons why you must make it happen no matter what. When patterns are broken, new worlds emerge. Energy favours champions, especially those who are disengaged from worn out barriers and act unconventionally, against their own standards. Keep your spirits high and believe that you already have within you all that is required to see it through. Belief is the thermostat that regulates what we accomplish in life. Belief will drive you to action. Belief combined with action creates miracles.

Ask yourself what is really important, and then have the wisdom and courage to build your life around that answer. Especially during those hard times, the person you become in the process will be a wonder to behold. The character that you built, the courage that you develop, the faith that you are manifesting will increase your deserving power.

Our inner-deserving power can be shaped by our conditioning and upbringing. Sometimes we stay stuck to our old ways, so much so that it becomes second nature and we do not recognise the necessity of moving on to different paths. By surrounding yourself with the right people and continually doing the inner work, you will be able to bring forth the desired changes.

Only a man who knows what it is like to be defeated can reach down to the bottom of his soul and come up with the extra ounce of power it takes to win when the match is even.
—Muhammad Ali

How big is your invisible container?

Your deserving power can be likened to a container that is designed to catch rainwater. To catch water, you need two things. First, you need the rain to come and, second, you need the ability to capture all the water. The amount of rainwater that you are able to catch is in direct proportion to the size of the container. The questions is: how big is your container? The most important ingredient to becoming successful and breaking into Quadrant 4, more important than a great idea, more important than hard work, is doing the inner work to increase your invisible container, your deserving power. If we don't do this work, we sabotage ourselves.

Studies show a common phenomenon. When tracked over a ten-year period, 80 per cent of lottery winners who win vast sums of money end up in the same financial situation as they were prior to the win. In most cases, there was no expansion of that invisible spiritual container. Their container was not large enough to accept and assimilate that much abundance. The excess that exceeded their intrinsic sense of deserving simply spilled over the sides.

A casting director client once shared that they had seen many talented but unknown actors blow an audition once they got in the room with a Hollywood director who had the power to transform their career. Because the stakes were high, and outside the range of the actor's comfort zone (or deserving zone), they unconsciously sabotaged the meeting by being overly nervous or not memorising the lines in order to place themselves in an advantageous position ahead of the competition.

Equally and oppositely we hear stories of great entrepreneurs who become devastating close to losing everything materially and, in some cases, do lose everything materially, only to find a few years later they are back on top. Their intrinsic deserving power is vast and, therefore, magnetises into their invisible container which they desire. They keep pressing because they understand that the tough times don't last but tough people do. They are thankful for the struggle because, without it, they would not have stumbled upon their strength.

When you know who you are and you are solidly aligned in your truth, people don't know what to do with you, or how to act around you because you are not easily influenced, swayed or manipulated.

The bottom line is this: if we don't do the inner work to increase our deserving power, we think small. Small thinking creates small results. To create big results we need big thinking – and to create big thinking, we need to increase our deserving power. We need to expand that invisible internal container to hold more of what we want.

If you keep going on in life and see all the opportunities that the universe places in front of you as 'too good to be true', you are only setting up yourself for mediocre experiences. You do nothing to increase your deserving power.

In his book *The Obstacle is the Way: The Timeless Art of Turning Trials into Triumph,* Ryan Holiday argues that obstacles do not inhibit success; they create success. And how we respond to obstacles is what defines us. On the other side of the obstacle – whether we smash through it, jump over it, dig under it or run around it – is our pot of gold. Your problems are your life rewards.

So that problem, that thing you dread, the thing that you are losing sleep over and stressed about … what if it wasn't so bad? What if you can make yourself so big, so expansive, so elevated, that the problem becomes so small? And what if, embedded inside that obstacle, were benefits designed especially for you? The Universe will only hand to you that which it knows you can handle at any point in time. When you can truly grasp this concept, and when you can truly understand that the Universe will never let you face the dark night of the soul unless you already possess the tools to overcome, then you may think twice about consenting to playing small. It is then up to you whether or not to use these God-given tools and recognise that you are not a victim of consequence but the master of your destiny.

When we understand that 'the obstacle is the way', we understand that life doesn't happen *to* us – life happens *for* us. And when we understand the law of vibration, we understand that life can happen *from* us and *through* us. Rather than crying 'Why me?', we face the obstacle with grit and gratitude in our hearts, stating instead, 'Why not me?' And you will see, when the floodgates bust open and torrents of abundant opportunities, prosperity, love and success are unleashed, you will have a different reason to fall to your knees, and from your state of grace and open heartedness, you will find yourself crying, 'What on earth did I ever do to deserve so much?'

You may encounter many defeats, but you must not be defeated. In fact, it may be necessary to encounter the defeats, so you can know who you are, what you rise from, how you can still come out of it. —Maya Angelou

FOUR POWERFUL SPIRITUAL PRACTICES TO INCREASE YOUR DESERVING POWER

Spirituality can be explained in its entirety in one sentence: *To tame and conquer this mind and heart of ours.* Spirituality is the practice of transforming our hearts and our minds. Transforming your mind transforms your perceptions and your experiences. Your circumstances will change if your perceptions change. Everything is about perception.

In the following sections, I run through four fast and effective ways to tame your mind and your heart to increase your deserving power.

Meditation

Meditation means 'to become familiar with' – to become familiar with a more serene and flexible way of being. It is to become familiar with a joy for existence and a love of life.

Life for me is rarely about time management. Life for me is about energy management. As entrepreneurs, our energy is our most valuable resource, and meditation is my most powerful energy management tool. Meditation is my secret weapon. Often, I do not call it 'meditation'; for me it is 'mind training and heart training'.

Meditation has its roots in the contemplative practices of nearly every major spiritual religion. The belief in meditation's benefits coincides with recent neuroscientific findings showing that the adult brain can be deeply transformed through this experience. The goals of meditation, in fact, overlap with many of the objectives of clinical psychology, psychiatry, preventative medicine and education. Meditation is the cultivation of basic human qualities, such as a more stable and clear mind, emotional balance, a sense of caring and mindfulness, as well as love and compassion – qualities that remain latent as long as one does not make an effort to develop them.

Meditation is not about controlling your thoughts; it is to stop your thoughts controlling you

As suggested by a growing compendium of research, meditation can alter the neuroplasticity of the brain, helping to treat symptoms of depression, fear and anxiety, and improve sleep patterns. The cells in your body react to everything that your mind says. Negativity also brings down your immune system. All fear and anxiety comes from a mind that is untamed. The only thing you fear is fear itself. It is fear of an untamed mind. This is depression. Happiness is defined as a heightened state of emotion and is only subjective to one's experience and does not exist objectively. There is always hope.

Meditation helps us to cultivate a sense of overall wellbeing and deserving power. It is proven to increase the immune system, decrease blood pressure, increase heart function, decrease stress hormones and chronic pain. We also get better sleep, and are more calm and alert. You will also see significant improvements to your mood, your sex life and your work performance. People who meditate are energised and look radiant and youthful. Meditators also light up the lives of those around them because they possess what I call 'happiness without reason' or 'anticipatory joy' – a non-dual happiness that is not dependent on external circumstances.

When the going gets tough, meditation allows me to steady my nerves and face life's obstacles with dignity, grace and poise. Meditation has allowed me to learn the art of acquiescence – to find cheerfulness and compassion even in the darkest of times. When the going gets tough, meditation allows me to pause and think more intelligently so that I can harness creativity, innovation, inspiration, collaboration and imagination – the traits that lead to problem-solving – as opposed to being in a state of fight or flight. On a deeper level, if we calm our minds, we will conquer and transform our perceptions, and our circumstances and outer conditions will change.

We do not meditate to get good at meditation; we meditate to get good at life

Your meditation does not need to be complicated. It can be as simple as closing your eyes and going inward for ten to fifteen minutes a couple of times a day. Do this every day for two to three months and watch how your life changes. When we go inward, we tap into a vast unbounded ocean of consciousness that is our authentic nature. This timeless unbounded aspect of who we are transcends our conditioning and all of the perceived trials and tribulations of our life and upbringing.

Meditation helps us to go beyond the relative story that we have been telling ourselves about our life. As a result, our inner confidence and authentic power begins to grow. This eternal dimension that we tap into knows no boundaries or limits. Once we identify with this unbounded eternal aspect of our identity, our deserving power begins to expand. It expands because to our authentic self, no experience is too wonderful or too great to be had.

In my Awaken the Spiritual Entrepreneur program, we take the rules out of meditation. I am obsessed with making the profound seem simple. As an entrepreneur, I do not believe in regularly practising the type of renouncing meditation that requires you to disappear into a forest for weeks on end without speaking a word to anyone, eating nothing but lentils and sitting in meditation 24/7. It simply is not practical for the life of an entrepreneur. I prefer to attune my teachings to the everyday world, so that I can continue to effectively run my family, my businesses, my passion projects and my life while being in a state of inner peace and flow.

I have been fortunate to travel to many parts of our beautiful world and have observed the reality of people's lives. My methods are a combination of the very best techniques that I have learned from neuroscientists and spirituality teachers from all around the world. And I have translated these teachings with my own flavour to make the teachings relevant and effective while losing none of their authenticity, purity and power. To get you started, you can access some simple guided meditations on my website (www.paulinenguyen.com.au/meditations).

When the five senses and the mind are stilled, when the reasoning intellect rests in silence, then begins the highest path.
—The Katha Upanishad

Nature's medicine

Let's face it, being an entrepreneur can be an incredibly tough gig. There is stress and there is pressure. There are all sorts of issues and problems to deal with on a daily basis. We never seem to get a break from the seemingly unrelenting effects of stress on our lives. But there is a way to use stress to our advantage. The fact of the matter is that two types of stress are possible. There is the positive and motivating stress called *eustress* – where you experience excitement and the joy of engaging in competition. Then there is *distress* – where things are too difficult and too hard and create too much anxiety. So, as an entrepreneur, how do we effectively decompress?

Nature's medicine is one sure way to combat stress and increase our deserving power. Mother Nature has always looked after us. Did you know that trees are among the world's greatest healers? Studies from many countries, including Japan, Finland, and the United States, have shown that 'forest bathing' (the practice of going to the forest to receive mental and physical healing) as well as 'earthing' (the process of absorbing earth's free flowing electrons from its surface through the soles of the feet) can greatly reduce stress, increase joy levels, lower blood pressure, improve concentration, strengthen the immune system, build up vitality, and provide powerful anti-cancer benefits. Simply adding a fifteen-minute walk in nature to your daily routine has been known to decrease the risk of cancer by 40 to 50 per cent.

Several studies have documented that being in nature every day – whether it be jumping in the ocean, walking barefoot in the sand, watching the sunrise, counting the stars at night or simply cloud gazing – is one of the fastest ways to combat stress, depression, anxiety and overwhelm. Getting out in nature every day also relieves migraines, improves blood pressure, lowers the heart rate, reduces stress-hormone production and adrenalin, and provides preventative effects for hypertension. What a wonderful way to relieve these symptoms without heading for the drugs.

For the Spiritual Entrepreneur, being one with nature is an important part of how we do business. Three consecutive days in nature can increase our problem-solving skills by 50 per cent. Walking and increasing cognition in nature is the best way to learn or have a meeting – it makes us think outside the square. Movement activates the brain, and walking and talking in nature increases bonding and friendship.

Exercising in nature also provides unique benefits that positively impact our psychology, our brain, our mood and many other factors. Trees and plants omit essential oils called 'phytoncides'. Inhaling phytoncides activates our immune system and helps us fight colds and flus and other viruses and infections, and these effects can last up to one week.

And the benefits from nature can be found in all its states. In his book *Blue Mind*, Wallace J Nichols explores our emotional ties to water and writes that our brains are hardwired to react positively to water, and that being in and around water provides the most profound shortcut to happiness. He combines water science and neuroscience to show exactly that. Nichols explains the technology of brain study, contemplating what happiness is and how it is evaluated, and looking at the effect of the colour blue and the other sensations of water. Nichols explores the recreational use of water and the health benefits of water, including its therapeutic use for PTSD, drug addiction and autism. He defines the 'blue mind' as a mildly meditative state characterised by calm, peacefulness and unity, and a sense of general happiness and satisfaction with life. This state is inspired by water and the sensations associated with it.

My teacher, Buddhist monk Thich Nhat Hanh, describes nature's medicine splendidly:

> *In the Buddhist tradition that I am part of, we do a practice called 'touching the earth' every day. It helps us in many ways. You too could be helped by doing this practice. When you feel*

restless or lack confidence in yourself, or when you feel angry or unhappy, you can kneel down and touch the ground deeply with your hand. Touch the earth as if it were your favourite thing or your best friend.

The earth has been there for a long time. She is mother to all of us. She knows everything. The Buddha asked the earth to be his witness by touching her with his hand when he had some doubt and fear before his awakening. The earth appeared to him as a beautiful mother. In her arms she carried flowers and fruit, birds and butterflies, and many different animals, and offered them to the Buddha. The Buddha's doubts and fears instantly disappeared.

Whenever you feel unhappy, come to the earth and ask for her help. Touch her deeply, the way Buddha did. Suddenly, you too will see the earth with all her flowers and fruit, trees and birds, animals and all the living beings that she has produced. All these things she offers to you. You have more opportunities to be happy than you ever thought. The earth shows her love to you and her patience. The earth is very patient. She sees you suffer, she helps you, and she protects you. When you die, she takes us back into her arms.

With the earth you are safe. She is always there, in all her wonderful expressions like trees, flowers, butterflies and sunshine. Whenever you are tired or unhappy, touching the earth is a very good practice to heal you and restore your joy.

Movement

Movement is the most underrated factor for quality of life. You are a body. You must move. Movement is not just moving your body from one place to another – that's called transportation. It is the quality of your movement that is key. Exercise is a celebration of what your body can do. Not a punishment for what you ate. Give your body what it was created for. It was created to move. It was not made for sitting for ten hours in front of the computer or in the car, or on a couch. Lack of movement and physicality is the cause of so many health problems

– physically, emotionally and mentally as well. We have to counteract the detrimental effects of sitting all day by exercising. Exercise and movement has proven to alleviate depression, anxiety and overwhelm.

Longevity is an idea that has become important to many of us. We now know that, as a species, we all will live longer. As Spiritual Entrepreneurs, we need to be strong and fit and healthy to help people solve problems for the rest of our lives. We must be in our optimum state to do our best work. Exercise connects the spinal cord to the brain. We need to move. When you change your energy, you change your life. When our muscles get stronger, our brains get stronger. The speed at which you learn improves your success.

Some interesting research shows a fascinating link between exercise and mindfulness meditation. Exercise releases the BDNF – or brain-derived neurotrophic factor – protein, which influences the growth of new neurons in the brain. Meditation does this as well. A study was conducted with groups of women in a shelter who had experienced domestic abuse and extreme trauma. They discovered that exercising every day helped with their mental health, but combining a twenty-minute cardiovascular workout with a ten-minute meditation turbocharged their physiology as well as psychology.

Another important factor is *rest*. We must always try to balance exercise with some sort of recovery or regeneration into our day. You can be stressed doing whatever you're doing during the day – whether it be public speaking, writing a book, or crushing a business meeting or a great workout – but the mistake many people make is not giving themselves a break and making time for rest and recovery and regeneration between the stress to allow themselves to get better and allow their bodies to recover. You need this rest to allow the brain to consolidate the information and decide whether it's going to save the information to long-term memory or discard it. We need to incorporate more deliberate relaxation and regeneration into our lives, whether it is a nap or meditation, to make sure that we are recovering afterwards. Peak performance has an equation:

$$Stress + Rest = Growth$$

If we don't incorporate that rest element, we will get into trouble.

The secret to living well and living longer is eat half, walk double, laugh triple and love without measure. —Tibetan proverb

Journalling

Journalling is the process of taking ten to fifteen minutes a day to write down our thoughts and feelings. We sit with a blank page and simply write out in one stream of consciousness whatever comes to mind, and we do this without stopping. This becomes a practice of self-awareness and contemplation and can become incredibly cathartic and meditative. Don't try to think things up, just put things down. As we place our thoughts on paper, we can begin to detect over time themes around our mental commentary.

As we write it all down, we become more conscious of what we are telling ourselves from moment to moment and day to day. This gives us the ability to detect any suboptimal patterns of thinking and highlight them for deletion.

Once we start doing the inner work to expand our invisible container, we can create Quadrant 4 success with effortless ease, and without fighting, resistance or struggle. We naturally and happily find ourselves in the right place at the right time, capturing opportunities that we couldn't have consciously planned.

What such a man needs is not courage but nerve control
and cool headedness. This he can only get through practice.
—Theodore Roosevelt

In this modern time, the great suffering we have is mental suffering. Suffering of the mind. All fear and anxiety and suffering rises from the delusion of an untamed mind. Many have inner peace but they are financially broke. Others have outer abundance but no inner peace. The Spiritual Entrepreneur strives to live in Quadrant 4 – the place of inner peace and outer abundance.

The Spiritual Entrepreneur commits daily to spiritual practices in order to tame their mind and increase their deserving power. People often think that compassion is something for others. Compassion must be for ourselves first. When we fill our hearts with love and compassion and use the power of our breath and our beating heart to uplift the human spirit, this not only improves our health but also increases our personal power, elevating our business, our families and our lives.

Our purpose in this lifetime is to evolve, transform, expand our consciousness and assist others to do the same. Our purpose in this lifetime is to carry out our life's work and share it with the world – and to do it with joy. Our purpose in this lifetime is to continue the practice of looking within, for this is our true home. If we practice inner peace as a state of being enough times, it becomes our state of being. This is when the magic really starts to happen.

EMBRACE CHANGE, EXPECT CHANGE – BE THE CHANGE

The awakening of consciousness is the next evolutionary step for mankind. There's a shift happening in humanity, a shift in consciousness, happening now because it has to happen now.

—Eckhart Tolle

DISCOVERING THE 'NEW WAY', THE 'BETTER WAY'

Most entrepreneurs don't read spirituality books. The fact that you have read this book this far means that you are not like most entrepreneurs. The fact that you have read this far means that you have been paying attention. Unfortunately, many are still living under a rock and have been oblivious to the fact that we are all going through incredibly deep and powerful metamorphoses individually and collectively as a human species. Many have been oblivious to the increasing conversations happening in the world today around consciousness, quantum physics, mindfulness, meditation, manifestation, and anything about spirituality and spiritual practices. You are not one of them. The fact that you have read this far means you are part of a small percentage of the population who are dissatisfied with the status quo, and actually want to do something about it. You simply will not rest on your laurels and accept that your dreams and goals are destined to remain unfulfilled.

Many entrepreneurs are unhappy and disengaged with their businesses and their lives. If you asked most entrepreneurs, they would say their businesses keep them from their families and their families keep them from the businesses. Guilt, shame, stress, fatigue and regret are the feelings they experience most hours of their day. Many find that their big life goals do not inspire them. They feel trapped in a life that they did not imagine because they were sold a dream. The reality is most entrepreneurs don't have what it takes to pursue and live that dream, or if they have managed to make money, it has not made them happy.

If you are like most entrepreneurs, you are faced with many challenges and obstacles on a daily basis. Cash flow could be a problem, getting new business may not be easy, getting your teams to work effectively may be giving you a headache, or trying to get a better bottom line result in the business may be proving to be impossible. And if you are a serial entrepreneur like me, you are constantly attempting to go out into the world to find a need. You are either finding a solution to a problem, filling a need, answering a question, filling a void, dealing with a challenge or trying to serve people. All the while, you are trying to keep your family happy, your health in check, and remain inspired at the same time.

Let's face it: there is no business if you are not inspired by what you are doing. For many entrepreneurs, the burden of responsibility has weighed so heavily that they have sacrificed their mental, emotional and physical health, leaving them desperate and uninspired. The harsh truth is, without energy, vitality and inspiration, no drive exists to make the business sustainably viable.

I am a firm believer that you should only be an entrepreneur if you can't *not* be an entrepreneur. The fact that you have read to the final chapter of this book means that you are a Seeker who is walking the road less travelled. You are on your own personal journey of self-realisation. You are hungry to find the answers to the questions you have been asking most of your adult life. You are hungry to discover a new way of thinking and a new way of being, so that you can fulfil the greatest vision you hold of yourself. You understand that being a successful entrepreneur is simply not about obtaining work–life balance. You understand that life is so much more than that. You understand that life is about discovering that unique treasure – the golden key that unlocks your personal code of abilities to realise your infinite potential.

When you are fuelled by who you are, your spirit uplifts others. And when you are excited about who you are becoming, your mind and your heart is engaged to challenge your creativity, as you realise the enormous potential to rewrite your own destiny. You are not just a human being; you are a human 'becoming'.

I honour you for being a part of the small percentage of entrepreneurs who yearn to find a 'better way'. Just as the human race is going through its next evolution, so too is the business world. We are transitioning from an era that was all about high pain thresholds, hardship and exertion to one that is fuelled by purpose, fulfilment, inner peace, spiritual abundance, self-sustainability and joy. You don't need to apologise for walking away from an energy that no longer resonates with who you are. The more conscious you become, the better choices you make. It is a new paradigm that the business world has not seen before, and you, my friend, are an early adopter, a true way 'revealer'.

Throughout this book I have used science and spirituality to give you a framework of reference for why this information is relevant and so very important. Science is the new language of mysticism because science demystifies the mystical and bridges cultures and societies based on research and hard evidence. The most beautiful thing we can experience is the mystical. It is the source of all true art and science. Combining science and spirituality is the logical next step for our evolution – an evolution that will eventually occur for the entire western world. Albert Einstein is commonly quoted as saying, 'There are only two ways to live your life. One is as though nothing is a miracle. The other is as though everything is a miracle.' In ten years, these conversations will become the norm – and you will have been one of the visionaries.

SPIRITUALITY WITHOUT THE BULLSHIT IS POSSIBLE

When I first started my speaking career three years ago, I was adamant about maintaining the title of 'Spiritual Entrepreneur', because the research and data showed me where the collective consciousness was heading. I was obsessed with my soul's purpose to push humanity forward – to activate human potential and alleviate suffering. I was obsessed with showing people that spirituality without the bullshit was possible. Three years ago, I was laughed at and ridiculed by many. 'You'll never make it as a speaker,' they said. 'You can't mention the world "spirituality" to the corporates,' they told me. 'Entrepreneurs will laugh at your talks around consciousness, "sleepwalking" and meditation,' they mocked. 'The entrepreneurs will think it's woo woo and voodoo,' they laughed. The term 'sleepwalking' means you are going through life unconsciously. Almost like you are in zombie mode and accept that 'suffering' is how life is supposed to be. Being wakened from a slumber is not always welcomed by those clinging to the final moments of sleep.

I am no stranger to being made fun of. I have been made fun of all my life. Vivid memories of being teased in the school playground as a fresh four-year-old Vietnamese boat person still bring a smile to my face. The first to awaken are often disgraced long before they are embraced. You know the world is upside down when those who have enlightened, compassionate views and future visions are accused of borderline insanity, and are ridiculed and criticised for thinking positively and optimistically. I know that the illiterate of the 21st century will not be those who cannot read or write, but those who cannot unlearn the many lies that they have been conditioned to believe, and cannot seek out the hidden knowledge that they have been conditioned to reject. Just because you don't understand it yet, doesn't mean you should reject it. Just because you don't understand it yet, doesn't mean it is not real. People are always afraid of what they don't understand.

A short two years into my speaking career, I became one of the most booked speakers in Australia, and this is what I know. I know that audiences are not only ready to hear this information but also CRAVING it. Why? Because the old ways are simply not working for so many of them. The old ways still cause them so much pain. Many suffer quietly and silently on their own. The plethora of messages, emails, testimonials that I receive, as well as the personal connections that I have made after every keynote presentation that I deliver, have shown me that, without a shadow of a doubt, more and more individual souls yearn to live the new way, the better way. The Way of the Spiritual Entrepreneur.

Spiritual development is preparation for what's to come. As we explore our resistance, we gain awareness of our ignorance. One of the downsides is that we can get divorced from the crowd. We may no longer fit into the norm when we start to realise what we are truly made of. I have learned that you cannot force someone to comprehend a message that they are not ready to receive. Still you must never underestimate the power of planting a seed. Even though the conscious mind is asleep, the subconscious mind is awake. We must keep planting seeds. Whatever we plant in our subconscious mind and nourish with repetition and emotion will one day become a reality. Isn't it amazing, though, how all who see beyond the illusion all come back with the same message? When the evidence no longer supports the current story, it is time for a new story.

With the convergence of neuroscience, quantum physics and universal laws, we now have new, more empowering paradigms by which to live our lives. New discoveries in areas ranging from human evolution and genetics to the new science of neuro-cardiology (the bridge between the brain and the heart) have overturned 150 years of thinking when it comes to the way we see ourselves in the world. Now we know that we are intentionally 'wired' for extraordinary capabilities that have appeared rare and mystical in the past.

> *I have been a Seeker and I still am, but I stopped asking the*
> *books and the stars. I started listening to the teaching of my soul.*
> —Rumi

When the facts are clear, our choices become obvious

The new paradigms that I teach in my Awaken the Spiritual Entrepreneur program are based on this convergence of neuroscience, quantum physics and universal laws. With the understanding that you can change your body, reprogram your mind into freedom and recreate your reality, you have the power to change your business, your life and your societies. Quantum physics has created a second scientific revolution, and these new paradigms will soon become the new wisdom of your children and grandchildren.

And you won't have to wait until these new paradigms are universally adopted – you get to be an early adopter, and you get to experience right now how it feels to accomplish your goals and dreams more completely than you had hoped. You will be one of the first to ride this wave of transformation. You will be the groundbreaker, the leader in your field, because what you will learn will fill your heart with so much joy, and there will be so much love in your being-ness that the minor irritations of your old conditioning will no longer limit you. Awaken the Spiritual Entrepreneur will teach you how to access more energy

– more life force – and you will embody the willpower and resourcefulness to achieve the goals you once thought were unattainable.

To live an extraordinary life, we must become limitless

Rejecting the old ways of hardship and wasted exertion moves us away from pain and towards discovering our true selves. We awaken to ourselves. Alleviating pain and suffering for entrepreneurs has been my life's mission for the last ten years. But I realised I had to start with myself – with my own pain – in order to get past the abuse in my own childhood. I understood myself only after I destroyed myself. And only in the process of fixing myself did I discover who I really was. When you begin to awaken, layers will be shed, and you may experience rage, depression, anxiety and fear, but you must ride the wave of transformation. There is no reality except the one contained within us. That is why so many people live an unreal life. They take images outside them for reality and never allow the world within to assert itself. We are disturbed not by things but by the view which we take of them. Living only in the physical, mental and emotional realm makes energy limited. Tap into the spiritual dimension and the energy is limitless.

Growth can still be painful. Often it is the deepest pain that empowers us to grow into our higher self. Pain is inevitable, but transformation is by conscious choice. Aspects of ourselves die when we evolve spiritually. Allow the old to exit your system because your illusion self (your ego) is being heard. Create the space for more of your soul's energy so that your true self (your spirit) can thrive. My core conviction is that, no matter what events may have happened to us, our biography does not equal our destiny. Perhaps the hardest thing, and the greatest gift about this type of growth, is never seeing the world in the same way again. Regardless of where you start, how you finish is on you. You cannot build a reputation on what you are 'gonna' do. Embrace the transition.

Beautiful are those whose brokenness gives birth to transformation and wisdom.

THE NEW REVOLUTION IS QUANTUM

We are beginning to see the entire universe as a holographically interlinked network of energy and information, organically whole and self-referential at all scales of its existence. We, and all things in the Universe, are non-locally connected with each other and with all other things in ways that are unfettered by the hitherto known limitations of space and time. —Ervin László

In his book *Why Quantum Physicists Do Not Fail,* futurist Greg Kuhn explains the 'unity paradigm' of the second scientific revolution of quantum physics. This too is part of the new way. The unity paradigm represents a shift away from looking at the material world outside of you and what part of this outside world is causing you to feel a certain way or experience certain results in your life. The science of the second scientific revolution shows us that the outside world is created by one's inside world, not the other way around. Your internal energy creates the material world outside of you. Embracing this paradigm as the scientific next step, as weird as it may sound to you right now, is as logical for humanity as embracing the earth's revolution around the sun was for a person in the 17th century.

Kuhn reveals that, when you study the science of the second scientific revolution, you will learn that the entire universe is actually an unformed field of energy called the quantum field.

The Quantum Field is a non-local and unbounded energy field representing all possibilities because it has no definite form yet — in layman's terms, it is everywhere all at once, it is endless and uncontained and it can become literally, anything. In other words, the Quantum Field is a mass of energy with the potential to form anything. All physical matter is manifested from the Quantum Field. This field waits in its state of infinite possibility for you to manifest the material world from it — which you do either deliberately or accidentally every second of every day you're alive.

Every creation begins as a thought. When we have an intention, a complex chain of events begins in our brains. Thoughts travel

as electrical impulses along neural pathways. When neurons fire together they wire together, creating electromagnetic fields. These fields are invisible energy, yet they influence the molecules of matter around us the way a magnet organizes iron fillings. The material world does not pre-exist awaiting your observation, you create the material world through your observations on a moment by moment basis.

If your inner energy and your inner thoughts are creating your material reality, isn't it of the utmost importance to manage the inner energy and manage the inner thoughts to create the results you want and the dreams you desire? And since we now know this, we can embrace the unity of you and the material world that you are creating right now. This new paradigm sets you free from limiting beliefs of old – that your actions are the only source of change.

Time and space are not conditions in which we live, but modes in which we think. —Albert Einstein

You have to lose your human mind to gain your spiritual senses

Herein lies the paradox. If you want more of whatever it is you desire, you have to first prove to the universe that you are capable of having it by developing a consciousness that affirms there is no shortage of it. The only way to do this is by creating a vacuum or space for what you desire to be received, and the only way you can create a space for it is by letting go of what you do have, trusting that the Universe knows what it is doing.

You have to believe first to see, not see first to believe. As Deepak Chopra argues,

There has been a revolution in how we perceive the body. What appears to be an object, a three-dimensional anatomical structure, is actually a process, a constant flow of energy and information.

You are a powerful being. If you had the power to unconsciously create the mess that you are in, you have the power to consciously fix it. If you had the power to unconsciously give yourself this dis-ease, you have the power to consciously heal yourself. If you had the power to unconsciously become the person you are today, you have the power to consciously design the person you want to become tomorrow.

ALWAYS SEE THE BIG PICTURE: IT IS AN EXCITING TIME TO BE ALIVE

But there is one phenomenon which, for some reason, we try with all our might to avoid. Desperately to avoid! One gets the impression that we are afraid to talk about it. We are afraid, I say, because it could so easily knock the wind out of our commonly accepted system of education and scientific deductions and make a mockery of the object inherent in our lifestyle! And we try to pretend that such a phenomenon does not exist. But it does! And it will continue to exist, however much we try to turn away from it or avoid it. Isn't it time to take a closer look at this and, just maybe, through the collective effort of all our human minds together, find answers to the following questions? —Vladimir Megre, *Anastasia: The Ringing Cedars Series, Book One*

You will recall in Secret #1 that an important element for Spiritual Entrepreneurs was to always see the big picture. There is always a much bigger picture at play.

Humanity has lived in unconsciousness for many lifetimes and could not evolve much further using the mind alone. This is changing. As already mentioned in this chapter, millions are awakening and no longer want to live the old ways. They do not wish to live under the manipulation and control of these old ways. And because the collective consciousness is rising, so too is the vibration of the planet. We are literally raising the vibration of our planet together. And this means the old energies of manipulation and control, which are lower frequency energies – with people functioning from deep unconsciousness, which is the level of greed and power — can no longer control and manipulate the awakened.

A prophesised acceleration in technology and consciousness is currently occurring — right on time with what has been decoded from Mayan information and ancient prophecies. It is a gradual process in the consciousness shift that is going on. It is an awakening, a step forward in consciousness. We are at what the Mayan prophecy says is the time of harvest, the time of the end. Not the end of the world but the end of suffering. The end of the wave of evolution of humankind when certain ones awaken and remember who they are and reclaim their divinity.

Those who have been paying attention will know that we are experiencing a kind of wave right now in building consciousness and it is about to turn into a tsunami of awareness. A shift is happening. What is occurring on our earth is at the leading edge of creation and the Universe is watching. This beautiful awakening is definitely not something that we should have any fear about. Things are not going to get worse; they are going to get uncovered. There is great excitement now because humanity's awakening is in progress. The world's people are waking up from the spell. Transformation is under way regardless, within you, right now, as we speak and as you read this. It is real. Trust it. Honour it. Nurture it. Cultivate it. Protect it.

Just as a computer would have to have the ability to modify its own programming to become self-aware, a human seeking self-awareness needs to be able to do the same — modify their own programming. This is the shift that is happening now. We are modifying our own programming.

With so much disruption taking place, the old society will not be the same. People don't believe in the old system anymore. We are no longer chasing the so-called dream that we have been brainwashed to believe. We are actually doing what our inner self dictates to us. People are starting to become aware of who they are, and starting to realise that there is more to life. And they really do want more — not in terms of material things but more in terms of peace and love and no more suffering. People are starting to realise that a community and humanity is out there.

There is a great excitement now for what is occurring, and what is about to become, and your role in self-transformation plays an important part. When you change your bodies and reprogram your mind into freedom, you can change your societies – which leads to the transformation of humanity, which leads to the transformation of the whole universe. This may be hard for the mind to accept, but it is the case.

Quantum physicist Mohsen Paul Sarfarazi, PhD, indicates that:

> We have reached an era in human history that logic and physical consciousness through utilization of brain alone no longer serves humanity. It is time to open one's heart and polish one's intuitive senses so that one can self-reflect by connecting to one's HIGHER SELF or I AM presence, inhabiting in higher dimensions of consciousness.

The quantum field is not a place, it is everything. It is out of time – there is no time there. And when you connect your consciousness and merge with that quantum field, you start to know things that you haven't learned in the old ways. You start to access skills and abilities. You start to be able to receive from the wisdom of your past. You start to know what is about to occur in your immediate future because you can read the potentials.

THE ONLY THING TO FEAR IS FEAR ITSELF

> We are more often frightened than hurt; and we suffer more from imagination than from reality. —Lucius Annaeus Seneca

We know that we are at a time when people are ready to awaken and adopt a new way, when a great transition will take place. An awakening of consciousness is the next step forward in our evolution. Society as we know it now is changing rapidly. All shall benefit on different levels because that is how the Universe elevates souls. People are becoming more conscious of the fact that we need to change our habits and take responsibility. We have to go along with the change that is happening as opposed to fear it and resist it. When we go into fear and loathing our bodies shut down. It is possible that those who are in that frame of mind will be left behind.

It is a choice right now between fear and love. Mohsen Paul Sarfarazi, PhD, further explicates that:

Fear is the most devastating enemy of man, an instrument of the captors of the man within this duality-infested matrix of reality, which we are imprisoned in, presently. As the age of ascension is upon us, it is of utmost importance that humanity, once and for all, abandons fear all together in search of his/her true inner divine identity.

One of the first things we are subject to is fear. Your fears are deep rooted. The first step is to acknowledge these fears and the depth to which they go. If there is nothing to fear except fear itself and you drop that fear, you have to be in bliss. If you are intelligent, if you are alert, the ordinary becomes the extraordinary. You can pierce the illusions of matter, and become conscious that you are divine. Bliss is our birthright. We were made to enjoy love and happiness. That bliss is always there. There is so much potential for bliss. It's like a light switch. You know that when you turn a switch on, the light comes on and the room fills. That's what bliss is like. It is there waiting for you to turn it on and you can tap into it as much as you want.

Dawson Church describes his bliss beautifully, and the following passage brings a tear to my eye each time I read it:

Sometimes right in the middle of an ordinary day, the beauty of life hits me like a cloudburst. I stop in my tracks, overwhelmed, tearful, too stunned to be able to take it all in. I stop what I'm doing and allow the feeling to expand. I open my heart big enough to stretch around the full extent of my blessings. I relish

those moments, savouring them as I expand my sense of self to
accommodate the full measure of life's beauty and perfection.
A life lived in conscious synchronicity with the universe is a life
well lived.

LOVE IS THE GLUE OF THE UNIVERSE.

You have heard before that 'love is the key' and you have put it away in your mind. And what is the opposite of love? It is not hate. Fear is the opposite of love, and it is your fears that have you holding on to what is, rather than allowing the natural flow of existence. This is why I stressed again and again in Secret #5 that love dissolves fears. With love, you start feeling your inner strength, start knowing that whatever happens, 'I will be beautifully fine. Whatever happens, I can handle it.' And then the mind might bring up stories from your past and other people's past – 'Oh, how difficult it is.' And then you go back into the fear again. Catch yourself. Be aware of your addiction to fear. The more one loves and finds unity in this world and harmony, the more the blessings will be when that time comes.

Have faith to trust in love, to choose in love and that will end up taking you to a much better place. The more responsible we become for our actions, the more harmonious the world will be. If you continue to operate out of fear and continue to operate through the ego, you will continue to be controlled and you will continue to not have a clue about what's going on in the world around you – or even inside you for that matter.

When you become aligned with who you truly are, you come from that place of knowingness, and from that place of knowingness comes so much potential for you to change this beautiful planet and, more importantly, to change your own experience on this earth. When you choose love, you love yourself more. Loving yourself is the greatest gift that is possible to give to the whole of your humanity.

KNOW THYSELF, HEAL THYSELF, LOVE THYSELF AND BE FREE

Reality is ultimately a selective act of perception and interpretation. A shift in our perception and interpretation enables us to break old habits and awaken possibilities for balance, healing and transformation. —David Simon

When we awaken fully, we are so much in control of our destiny it is unbelievable, and yet billions are persuaded they are not, and therefore they create a very different reality. So, if we are in fear, we can attract the reflection of fear. The fear is a lack of being all powerful and so being anything less than an infinite love puts us into a state of fear. Again – one of the first things we are subject to is fear. This is the greatest stick you can give to anyone to control a human being. It is called slavery. If a person doesn't have freedom from fear, they are some sort of a slave. A slave to themselves. Our consciousness is controlled. As people begin to awaken and take on responsibility for their own evolution, we can expect to see a much more harmonious world.

When we open up and become a part of this transition and accept it, we will be a part of an amazing transformation that is getting ready to occur. If you have been paying attention, you will realise that, as entrepreneurs who want to make a positive impact on our future and the future of those around us, we have to go along with the change that is happening – as opposed to fearing it and resisting it. Let go. Let go of how you thought your life should be and embrace the life that is trying to work its way into your consciousness. It is an amazing time in history to be alive. Don't get left behind.

The more we become the more we attract. The more we attract, the more we awaken. There is an old saying that an enlightened being plays with the Universe the way that a child plays with a ball – because they see the reality of everything, they can't be tricked, they can't be fooled. A person who is awakening and becoming enlightened cannot be controlled. Someone who cannot be controlled is fearless, stress free and unshakable.

This is the Way of The Spiritual Entrepreneur.

YOU ARE NEVER ALONE

Being spiritual has nothing to do with what you believe and everything to do with your state of consciousness. I cannot tell you any spiritual truth that deep within you don't already know. All I can do is remind you of what you have forgotten.
—Eckhart Tolle

If nature is made of nothing but unconscious matter, how are we conscious? There is a larger consciousness of which we are all part. It is no coincidence that the endemic disease in modern industrial society is depression. Spiritual practices such as meditation, prayer, invocation, chanting, singing and dancing can actually help with all of this. Even more so, when we can find our 'soul tribe' or our 'soul colleagues', our lives are made all the more fun, fulfilling and richer.

When we say, 'I am a Spiritual Entrepreneur, and I am doing some kind of spiritual practice and follow spirituality,' what it means is, 'I am finding out who I truly am.' I am asking the important questions. What am I? Who am I? Where did I come from? What am I doing here on this Earth? Why did I come? Where will I go? What will I do? Who will I choose to become? Who am I meant to play with in this game called life?

The community of Spiritual Entrepreneurs that we have built allows lonely entrepreneurs to tap into an authentic community of like-minded businesspeople to supercharge their energy, ideas, imagination, creativity, inspiration and vitality. You can surround yourself with inspired souls who are on the same journey to live a better, more charged life. When you connect with inspired entrepreneurs who have a conscious heart and a sharp mind, the conversation is different and you cannot help but be uplifted.

When you are in the energy field of spirituality, people feel transformed by your presence without a word being spoken – they share the energy field that you inhabit and you feel uplifted. While connected in powerful resonance patterns with the field produced by meditation, you participate in that energy. And you are never alone because you will have the needed support in those moments when you feel overwhelmed, when it feels like the world has so many troubles. We can support you in those moments of sadness and struggle, not only in the realm of the senses but also through the quantum connection.

Matthew Kelly, in his book *The Rhythm of Life*, put it beautifully:

> *The people we surround ourselves with either raise or lower our standards. They either help us to become the best-version of ourselves or encourage us to become lesser versions of ourselves. We become like our friends. No man becomes great on his own. No woman becomes great on her own. The people around them help to make them great. We all need people in our lives who raise our standards, remind us of our essential purpose, and challenge us to become the best-versions-of-ourselves.*

And when you fall, and you can pick yourself up each time and surround yourself with a strong support system, you will find your measure of success.

Join our community of Spiritual Entrepreneurs at the next Awaken the Spiritual Entrepreneur Retreat. Here you will discover a safe space where you can share your challenges and burdens as well as your goals and dreams. Here you will find your own conscious group of people who provide not only business support but also spiritual support – connecting together for the common purpose and providing inspiration to bring your business and projects alive with heart, soul and Universal Flow.

In his book *Mind to Matter*, Dawson Church describes this state powerfully:

> *When you are in alignment with the Universal Flow, the Quantum Field unlocks before you alignment with all the synchronicity, grace, beauty, and wisdom of the Universe. Horizons of creativity open up to you, and you are in flow. You know yourself to be one with Universal Wisdom, with Universal Power, with Universal Intelligence, with Universal Love. From that place of consciousness, you live a life of wisdom, intelligence, and love. You no longer ask for love, need love, or crave love because you*

are love. You no longer pray for wisdom, because you are wisdom. You no longer seek inner peace, because your very nature is peace. Standing in that place, you have access to all the wisdom, peace, and love in the universe.

It is the state we are meant to live our lives in all the time. It's been perceived as a special, occasional exception to the grind of daily life. Yet it's meant to be the way we start and end each day. Each day is meant to flow in an unfolding of synchronous possibilities. And you living in attunement with the universal field has an entirely different sense of self than a you living as a self-isolated local mind. Perceiving yourself as one with this synchronized universe, you move into your day with a sense of equanimity, power, peace, joy, love exuberance.

Suddenly, you are no longer an isolated individual bumping into this or that problem or challenge. Instead, when you are in tune with Universal Flow, you are a part of an orchestra of synchronised movement. You are one with the Universe, and you are one with everyone else who is one with the Universe. You are one with every force and phenomenon in nature that is also one with the Universe. When you are one with the Universe, you dance in tune of the natural harmonics of creation.

Spirituality is a way of life, pure and original as given by the most high. Spirituality is a network linking us to the most high, the Universe and each other. —Haile Selassie I

Embracing the Law of Reciprocity

When your actions are based in the perception that everything and everyone on earth is connected – that you are not an isolated individual dealing with problems and challenges alone – it is inevitable that you will create a level of success in every area of your life. Success that soars above and beyond what you are currently demonstrating. When you ask the important questions, you will receive the important answers. You will learn that you are not limited to this body, to this mind, or to its reality. You are a limitless ocean of consciousness, imbued with infinite potential. You are existence itself.

The need to belong is a universal emotion that is found across all cultures. Whether it is with family, friends, co-workers, religion, country or culture, we all share an inherent need to belong to something greater than ourselves. When we give and do good turns, a law is activated called the Law of Reciprocity. The support we gain from others is in direction proportion to the support we offer others.

Miraculously, the support reciprocated may not necessarily return from the individual you assisted; it may come from a complete stranger or the community at large. In eastern philosophy, this phenomenon is referred to as the Law of Karma. Karma is the chain reaction or the ripple effect of our actions. What we reap is a consequence of what we sow.

Imagine once more that two versions of you exist: A and B. You are identical in every way. You both have the same education, the same upbringing and the same level of ambition; however, version A of you looks for ways to serve customers beyond the financial return, and B does everything predominately with a view to get the financial return. Ironically you would discover that you A will outperform you B, in every conceivable way. You A would be wealthier not only in terms of dollars but also in happiness, health and satisfaction. The aim of the Spiritual Entrepreneur is to look not only at the bottom line but also for ways to bring a depth of meaning to each transaction with our customers that transcends the dollars and cents. When we lovingly take action to help our customers in fulfilling their goals and needs, we find that we become wealthy beyond our imaginings.

Over the many years of studying the science of Quadrant 4 success, I have found that there is one common denominator with those who enter and remain in Quadrant 4. This common denominator is something that is not only a theme among these Quadrant 4 dwellers, but is also absolutely necessary and a not negotiable personality characteristic. The common denominator is this: they are ALL great givers. They are in service to others. They give to their friends, they give to their family, and they give to their community. Without fail, Spiritual

Entrepreneurs in Quadrant 4 give of their time and attention as well as their money, and they are some of the most generous people you will ever meet. It is impossible to be happy and stingy at the same time.

What sets human beings apart from animals is, therefore, not the pursuit of happiness, which occurs all across the natural world, but the pursuit of meaning, which is unique to humans. People who have meaning in their lives, in the form of a clearly defined purpose, rate their satisfaction with life higher even when they are feeling not so great than those who did not have a clearly defined purpose.

CHANGE IS THE ONLY CONSTANT

The secret to change is to focus all of your energy not on fighting the old but building the new. —Dan Millman, *Way of the Peaceful Warrior*

Finally, and perhaps most importantly, adopting the new way means embracing change. A common theme that I come across in my coaching of entrepreneurs is their fear of change. I have assisted many in shifting their consciousness toward change. It is a joy to witness when they eventually grasp and accept the concept that change is the only constant. Change is a part of life. Change is life. We are not separate from it. In fact, we are a part of it. Change happens instantly. What takes a long time and causes anxiety is the hesitation, the 'umming and ahing' and going backwards and forwards before you actually allow the change to happen. The painful part is the holding on when you know that it is time for change. Change itself is easy and beautiful. The fears that you create yourself beforehand and the holding back are what cause stress and fear. Change is natural. Change is part of this reality and yet we have been programmed that greatness is an exhausting task. You will know that you are resisting the call of the new way, however, when you constantly feel exhausted.

There is a simple truth – as you let go of the energy of the old reality the Universe will bring in the new. All space must be filled with a frequency – created over so many lifetimes to be in control. This programming has made us fear the uncertain future. And it is this controlling nature that slows down our natural process of evolution.

Change is simple and easy. What is extremely difficult for some of us is holding onto the old when the new wants to happen. Struggling to maintain that limitation when the change wants to happen is difficult. Pushing it down. Pushing it down. Stop pushing down at energy that wants to be free, especially when what it really wants is to come up. That is what takes your energy; that is what makes you tired and exhausted and fed up with living. There is nothing more exhausting than not living up to your full potential. Holding back your blessings and energy. Each energy field that is emptied must be re-filled. You have the power to choose the new energy frequency. Allow for the possibility that change can happen simply and easily. Be open to the possibility that change can happen effortlessly for you.

Allow the change. Allow everything to be in flux because it is. Allow things to be as they are. Allow your friends to come and go. Allow your homes to come and go. Allow your partners to come and go – they may be with you for a week, a month, a year, a lifetime or many lifetimes, but allow the flow. Allow change to be. It is the nature of reality. Let go. Let go of how you thought your life should be and embrace the life that is trying to work its way into your consciousness. Not only will you free yourself by embracing change, but you will also empower yourself by expecting change. Life then gets very exciting when you commit to Be the Change.

You don't need to change the whole world. If you start with changing yourself, you have already started changing the whole world. If even a single human being changes, that change will radiate to thousands and thousands of others. You will become a triggering point for a revolution that can give birth to a totally new kind of human being.

Adopting the Law of Detachment can accelerate our natural process of evolution. As Deepak Chopra tells us,

In detachment lies the wisdom of uncertainty, in the wisdom of uncertainty lies the freedom from our past, from the unknown, which is the prison of past conditioning. And in our willingness to step into the unknown, the field of all possibilities, we surrender ourselves to the creative mind that orchestrates the dance of the Universe.

When you know where we are going, you know what to take with you. More importantly, you will know who you need in your orbit to get you to your destination faster. As you awaken you will come to understand that the journey isn't about finding the one – it is about becoming the one. The ones who have changed will change everything. When you choose to embrace change, expect change and be the change, this is when you can truly become fearless, stress free and unshakable in this rapidly changing world.

RECAP AND NEXT STEPS

Here are the seven secrets I've outlined in this book:

- Secret #1: Redefining happiness
- Secret #2: Fulfilment is the new currency
- Secret #3: Be a contagion
- Secret #4: Unlearn everything – redesign your destiny
- Secret #5: Know thyself, heal thyself, love thyself
- Secret #6: Inner peace, outer abundance
- Secret #7: Embrace change, expect change – BE THE CHANGE

I trust you have now begun to understand, if you're not already implementing, these seven important secrets. And while you have reached the end of this book, the truth is that this is only the beginning of an incredibly exciting journey for you. It is a journey I am convinced you cannot afford to not take. The personal toll and the overall price of not taking this path are extraordinarily high. I have experienced this personal toll firsthand. I wish I had known these secrets many years ago, but I have accepted that it was not my time. I have accepted that we are a part of a greater wisdom than we'll ever understand, a higher order that has divine timing.

When I look back, I realise that my biggest mistake was accepting that I had to go through so much pain to get 'there'. I thought it was the way it was meant to be. Why did I go through so much pain to 'get there', when the 'there' is nowhere near as good as I am now!

Many of us have paid a handsome price to get there, and you will discover (if you haven't already) it is not worth it, as many others before you have discovered. It is a horrible realisation and feeling of emptiness when you arrive at your destination, only to realise you are still remarkably unfulfilled and unhappy, no matter the size of your bank account and material possessions.

Choosing to become a Spiritual Entrepreneur is not about shunning these goals or financial rewards, either. It is about making sure that when you get there, your life is full and harmonious – not broken, lonely and empty. This is a price so many have paid in their single-minded, misguided approach to achieving their misguided goal.

The pursuit of fame, money, power, status, titles and material possessions rarely brings what most people expect. External achievements will not fill your basic needs as a human being. Chasing these achievements without first striving for fulfilment and lasting happiness internally simply does not work. If you are not sure, ask anyone who has tried … and failed!

You didn't come here to chase money, status, fame or power; you came here to awaken to your true nature as spirit incarnate. When you seek lasting happiness through pursuing impeccability, integrity, fulfilment, love, trustworthiness, compassion, kindness and humility, whole new dimensions appear before you. Dimensions that can never be bought by money alone.

One way or the other, most people sooner or later realise they are not living the life they truly aspire to live. Most people who are trying to achieve success externally are either living in the past or the future, and so are missing out on the now, where life needs to be lived.

This is what so many entrepreneurs do – sacrificing today, delaying gratification for tomorrow or ten years down the road, so they may one day live the life of their dreams. What they don't realise is that they have the opportunity to live that life now. We don't have to repeat the mistakes of those who have gone before us. Our happiness, our success, nearly every detail of our lives comes down to choice, and we can choose to live the way we truly want to live, or spend our final days regretting the choices we didn't make.

Are you guilty of this? Are you chained to a certain life and to achieving goals that others in your society expect of you? Have you been indoctrinated by the system, your parents, your culture, religion and schooling to follow a path that is not true to you? Even if you have, you might not know it, unless you recognise these feelings within yourself currently – discontentment, feeling torn, unhappy, unsettled, stressed and fearful perhaps?

If you can identify strongly or even faintly with any or all of this and you have a yearning for something more, it might be time to take a different path.

In order to live a truly inspired life with lasting happiness, we need to be connected to our source of energy and inspiration. We need to take this connection and use it to manifest our OWN happiness and to improve every aspect of our lives. If we have the courage to take the first small step, our lives will inevitably transform.

THE WAY OF THE SPIRITUAL ENTREPRENEUR

You are what you think. What you think you will become. And if we are what we think, then I think we would be advised to hold the most positive and grand view that we can possibly have because what you think about is what you're going to create.

So how is this achieved? There are many ways. The fastest way is by following the seven secrets of this book and joining my Awaken the Spiritual Entrepreneur program.

The Way of the Spiritual Entrepreneur is a gift you give yourself. A gift that brings a whole new spiritual approach to becoming a more successful entrepreneur in every meaning of the word – not only outwardly but also, and more importantly, inwardly.

The Way of the Spiritual Entrepreneur is the path to transform your life from existence and struggle to peace, balance, harmony, joy, fulfilment and lasting happiness, without sacrificing your business, your relationships, or your health.

Enough knowledge is in this book to completely transform your personal and professional life for good. These seven secrets are holistic and congruent to the Way of the Spiritual Entrepreneur, designed to transport you to a new level of sustainable success.

Happiness, love, money, health, freedom and abundance are yours for the taking once you align yourself with your highest purpose for being. My definition of abundance is having everything you need when you need it, plus a little more to share with others. And when I say, 'Have what you need, when you need it', I don't just mean bread and water; I mean Quadrant 4 abundance – delightful meals, a beautiful place to live, a vacation when you need it. A comfortable vehicle to drive. Abundance in loving relationships. Abundant contribution to your community. It is time to claim this for yourself. It is time to go deep in those limitations and release them.

In the past you may have felt it is impossible to change, or that luck or being born in a rich family is required. Or perhaps you condemned change because it was the way you were brought up. The past must be left in the past. The past is no longer real. On the other side of fear is freedom and freedom does not have to be the goal. Freedom can be part of the journey.

This is a time in history when it is not enough to know. This is a time in history when we must know *how*. This book and the Awaken the Spiritual Entrepreneur retreat program teach you how.

The Awaken the Spiritual Entrepreneur retreat is designed for intelligent people who are willing to let go of the overriding fear of lack, and are willing to step into the unknown. The intelligent people who will watch as some in society move further into collapse, chaos and fear while they ride the wave of productivity, change, celebration and elation, feeling energised and full of hope for humanity. The intelligent people who are willing to say, 'I am going to let go of all my fears and allow something totally new transform me.' What we are offering is transformation through deep peace. What we are offering is freedom from suffering. What we are offering is the joy for existence.

We are here and we are ready.

Are you?

In love, wisdom and gratitude,
Pauline

To join me at Awaken the Spiritual Entrepreneur Retreat, please visit: www.paulinenguyen.com.au/ase

Life will never be the same again.

Other next steps include the following:

- *My speaking engagements:* I love being a Professional Speaker. Uplifting, inspiring and transforming as many people as possible in a short period of time was what I was put on this earth to do. I like to leave everyone I touch with a sense of increase. If you would like me to speak at your next event or teach at your next workshop, please get in touch at www.paulinenguyen.com.au/speaker/. You can also find plenty of awesome testimonials there!

- *One-on-one coaching and mentoring:*
  For enquiries in this area, please visit:
  www.paulinenguyen.com.au/coaching/.
  You'll find plenty of testimonials there too!

- *Enjoy my transformative guided meditations at:*
  www.paulinenguyen.com.au/meditations

- *At my restaurant:* And if you are in Sydney, please visit us for an uplifting experience, or book your next private function or event at Red Lantern, the most-awarded Vietnamese restaurant in the world: www.redlantern.com.au.